The Education of Asian and Pacific Americans:

Historical Perspectives and Prescriptions for the Future

Edited by Don T. Nakanishi and
Marsha Hirano-Nakanishi

ORYX PRESS
1983

The rare Arabian Oryx is believed to have inspired the myth of the unicorn. This desert antelope became virtually extinct in the early 1960s. At that time several groups of international conservationists arranged to have 9 animals sent to the Phoenix Zoo to be the nucleus of a captive breeding herd. Today the Oryx population is over 400 and herds have been returned to reserves in Israel, Jordan, and Oman.

This collection was prepared for and developed by the ERIC Clearinghouse on Urban Education, Institute for Urban and Minority Education, Teachers College, Columbia University, New York, New York, with funding from the National Institute of Education (U.S. Department of Education) under contract number 400-77-0071.

Library of Congress Cataloging in Publication Data
Main entry under title:

The Education of Asian and Pacific Americans.

Includes bibliographical references and index.
Contents: The education of Asian and Pacific
Americans / Bob H. Suzuki—Shattering myths, Japanese-
American educational issues / Florence M. Yoshiwara—
Overview of the educational progress of Chinese-
Americans / Kenyon S. Chan and Sau-Lim Tsang—[etc.]
1. Asian Americans—Education—United States—
Addresses, essays, lectures. 2. Hawaiians—Education—
Hawaii—Addresses, essays, lectures. I. Nakanishi,
Don T. II. Hirano-Nakanishi, Marsha.
LC3015.E38   1983   371.97'95'073   82-22257
ISBN 0-89774-030-0

Table of Contents

Preface

Asian and Pacific Americans are the subjects of numerous articles, mono-graphs, and books in the specialized fields of the social sciences as well as in the mass media. Like all ethnic groups, Asian and Pacific Americans have already stamped American society and will continue to add to its cultural diversity. Like other minority groups, Asian and Pacific Americans have also endured a sometimes painful acculturation, racial discrimi-nation, misunderstanding, stereotyping, and neglect.

Asian and Pacific Americans themselves point to problems that cur-rently impair their achievement of equity within the larger society. They are too often stereotyped as the "model" or "successful" minority, a percep-tion that allows society to neglect their needs with a clear conscience. There is also the tendency to cast the numerous and diverse Asian and Pacific American ethnic groups into one mold and ignore the differences that engender divergent problems and needs.

In recognition of these concerns and others affecting the education of Asian and Pacific Americans, the ERIC Clearinghouse on Urban Educa-tion, with funds from the National Institute of Education (U.S. Department of Education), commissioned the series of papers in this volume. As one of the 16 specialized clearinghouses in the ERIC (Educational Resources Information Center) system, a national information network, this Clearing-house is responsible for the field of urban and minority education. As one of its charges, it disseminates information about Asian and Pacific American education to teachers, educators, administrators, community workers, and laypersons interested or involved in education with these ethnic groups.

In April, 1980, members of the Clearinghouse staff attended the annual conference of the National Association for Asian and Pacific Ameri-can Education (NAAPAE) and asked for help in creating this volume; the articles for this book were completed in 1981 but were updated for this volume. From the outset we have sought Asian and Pacific American scholars to develop separate papers or essays concerning their own groups. NAAPAE has helped us identify these authors and has continued to assist us in identifying documents and other resources to support the development of this book, and individual members of the organization have also been instrumental in augmenting the amount of materials available through ERIC that deal with Asian and Pacific Americans.

We would like to especially acknowledge the following individuals for their invaluable assistance in the production of this book. Linda Wing, past President of NAAPAE and Director of the Asian American Bilingual Center in Berkeley, California, helped us conceive the thrust of each essay and lead us to authors for each of the essays; Jerome Wright, formerly Associate Director of the ERIC Clearinghouse on Urban Education, initiated the project and helped to nurture it. The following educators acted as reviewers and made invaluable suggestions for alteration in details and directions of the essays: Amy Agabayani, Tran Trong Hai, Yungho Kim, Gloria L. Kumagai, and Victor Low. Finally, we would like to thank Maryellen LoBosco, Editor at the Clearinghouse, who had the sometimes difficult task of coordinating editors, reviewers, authors, and publishers to bring this book to completion.

Erwin Flaxman, Director
ERIC Clearinghouse on Urban Education

Contributors

Bella Zi Bell has been Director of Research and Statistics at ALU LIKE, a social service agency serving the needs of Native Hawaiians in Hawaii, since 1976. Prior to that, she worked at the University of Hawaii, Honolulu, Hawaii; the East-West Center, Harvard University, Cambridge, Massachusetts; and overseas in various research positions and has conducted many demographic studies.

Kenyon S. Chan is currently Coordinator of Bilingual Education and Social Policy Studies at the National Center for Bilingual Research. Before taking this position, he was a professor in the Graduate School of Education at the University of California, Los Angeles. His most recent publications include articles on the effects of minority status culture and language on educational development and the socialization of children in school.

Marsha Hirano-Nakanishi is a research associate for the National Center for Bilingual Research at the Southwestern Research Laboratory. She is also president of the Asian American Education Commission, Los Angeles Unified School District.

Bok-Lim C. Kim is currently teaching part-time and consulting in program development and service delivery for limited English speaking Asian immigrants and refugees. She was formerly Associate Professor in the School of Social Work at the University of Illinois, Urbana, Illinois. She has served on the National Advisory Council on Bilingual Education for the Department of Health and Human Services and on the Presidential Commission on the International Year of the Child, 1981. Her major research and publications are in the area of Asian immigrants and their adaptation; her latest research is on the subject of the Korean immigrant children in the American public schools.

Federico M. Macaranas has been the Chairman of the Economics and Finance Department of Manhattan College, New York, New York, since 1979, where he also served as Director of the School of Business Research

Institute in 1977–78. He has written numerous articles and lectured extensively on economic issues in minority education and on the Filipino immigrant experience in the U.S. In addition, he writes regularly on developments in the Asian-Pacific economies. He has sat on panels of the National Institute of Education and has headed community organizations such as the Philippine Forum of New York. He is a member of the Community Advisory Board of the Pacific/Asian-American Mental Health Research Center (University of Illinois, Chicago Circle Campus).

Don T. Nakanishi is Assistant Professor at the Graduate School of Education, University of California—Los Angeles. He is co-founder and former publisher of *Amerasia Journal*. He has also conducted research on minority politics, political behavior, and Asian-American studies.

Bob H. Suzuki has been Dean of Graduate Studies and Research and Professor in the Department of Educational Foundations at California State University, Los Angeles, since January 1981. From 1971 to 1980, he was Assistant Dean and Professor in the School of Education at the University of Massachusetts, Amherst, Massachusetts. He has authored many articles on Asian Americans and education and is a specialist in the field of multicultural education. In addition to his scholarly pursuits, he has been actively involved for more than a decade in civil rights, social action, and community affairs; in 1976, he was honored as the first recipient of the National Education Association's Human Rights Award for Leadership in Asian and Pacific Island Affairs.

Vuong G. Thuy is a nationally recognized authority on the teaching of English to speakers of other languages (TESOL), bilingual education, and Indochinese education. Founder and first president of the National Association for Vietnamese American Education (NAVAE), Dr. Thuy is a recipient of many awards and has published extensively on TESOL, bilingual education, Indochinese education, parental involvement, and materials preparation. He has been a classroom teacher, university professor, lecturer, guest speaker, and presenter at nearly 200 international, national and regional conferences, seminars, symposiums and workshops on cross-cultural communication, bilingual education, TESOL, Indochinese education, linguistics, and materials preparation.

Sau-Lim Tsang is currently the Executive Director of ARC Associates, Inc., an educational research and development organization in Oakland, California. He formerly served as the Assistant Director of the Asian-

American Bilingual Center where he was instrumental in producing educational materials for limited English speaking Asian-American children.

Florence M. Yoshiwara is the General Manager of JACP, Inc. of San Mateo, California, which is the largest national disseminator of Asian-American educational materials. She is both a writer and developer of Asian-American curriculum materials, in print as well as nonprint; a consultant in Asian-American education, a college instructor; and she is currently serving as Secretary of the National Association for Asian-Pacific Education.

The Education of Asian and Pacific Americans: An Introductory Overview

by Bob H. Suzuki

According to the latest figures from the 1980 U.S. Census (Bureau of the Census, 1981), the number of persons categorized as "Asian and Pacific Islander" increased by a startling 128 percent, rising from 1.5 million in 1970 to over 3.5 million in 1980. During the same period, the Black population increased by 17 percent, the Hispanic population by 61 percent, and the Native American population by 71 percent, whereas the total population of the country increased by only 11.5 percent. Thus, the rate of growth of the Asian-Pacific American (APA) population was almost double that of the next fastest growing minority group and more than 10 times that of the U.S. population as a whole.

Partially due to this phenomenal growth in population, APAs are now being perceived as a minority group that will play an increasingly significant role in American society and will warrant much more attention than they have in the past. Consonant with this perception, the ERIC Clearinghouse on Urban Education at Columbia Teachers College commissioned this series of papers dealing with the APA population. The authors of the papers were asked to write for an audience of educational practitioners, administrators, and community groups; to discuss some of the fundamental issues affecting the education of various APA groups; and to dispel the misconceptions about APA groups that affect their equitable treatment in American society.

The following 6 papers were commissioned for the series: "Shattering Myths: Japanese-American Educational Issues" by Florence M. Yoshiwara; "Overview of the Educational Progress of Chinese Americans" by Kenyon S. Chan and Sau-Lim Tsang; "The Future of Korean-American Children and Youth: Marginality, Biculturality, and the Role of the American Public School" by Bok-Lim C. Kim; "Socioeconomic Issues Affecting the Education of Minority Groups: The Case of Filipino Americans" by Federico M. Macaranas; 'The Indochinese in America: Who Are They and How Are They Doing?" by Vuong G. Thuy; and "The Status of Native Hawaiian Education" by Bella Zi Bell.

As a reading of these papers will quickly reveal, there is tremendous diversity both among and within the various APA groups. This introductory overview will provide a descriptive framework to help readers of the papers discern common patterns and relationships among the multifaceted and seemingly unrelated experiences of these groups and, thereby, enable them to place the experience of each group into a broader, more understandable context. Concomitantly, when appropriate, certain important distinctions that should be made among or within these groups will be noted.

Drawing from the 6 papers listed above, as well as from other sources, and for the purpose of presenting this framework, the remainder of this overview is organized into 4 major sections: (1) a historical overview of the experiences of the various APA groups, placing emphasis on their patterns of immigration; (2) an analysis of the demographic characteristics of APAs; (3) a discussion of the educational problems and needs of APAs and some of the programs that have been mounted to address these problems and needs; and (4) some concluding comments on the papers and the future prospects for the education of APAs.

HISTORICAL OVERVIEW

Except for the Hawaiians who were the original settlers of Hawaii, all of the APA groups described in this collection were immigrants to an already populated land. As Bell notes in her paper, it is believed that the first Hawaiian settlers arrived from the Marquesas islands around 500 A.D. The immigration of the other APA groups, however, occurred in 2 fairly distinct phases: (1) the early immigration that took place between the late 1840s and 1934, and (2) the recent immigration that has occurred since 1965. During the 30-year period between 1934 and 1965, the United States allowed almost no immigration from Asia.

As the authors have chronicled in their papers, the first of the Asian immigrants, the Chinese, began arriving in the late 1840s. They were followed by the Japanese, the major proportion of whom arrived in Hawaii and the United States mainland between 1890 and 1924. Next to arrive, though in much smaller numbers, were the Koreans, who first came to the United States for a short period between 1903 and 1905. The Filipinos were the last of the Asian groups to arrive during this first phase of immigration, beginning to immigrate in the early 1900s and continuing to arrive until 1934. Most of these early Asian immigrants were poor peasants or small farmers, mostly young males, who tended to come from the more economically distressed areas of their respective countries.

Major contributions to the development of the American West and Hawaii were made by these early Asian pioneers. They provided much of the labor for the expanding agricultural industries of these areas and were largely responsible for building the vast network of railroads throughout the western states. Others worked in such fields as lumbering, fishing, and mining, and in jobs in canneries, domestic work, and gardening, in which the demand for cheap, unskilled, and dependable labor was high.

These contributions are especially impressive when considered in the light of the intense discrimination encountered by the early Asian immigrants. Not only did they arrive during a period when both racism and violence were rather commonplace in the American West, but also they were viewed as a competitive threat by White workers. Consequently, they became victims of countless repressive, often violent, acts of racism, including denial of citizenship, prohibition from testifying in court against Whites, discriminatory taxes, alien land laws, segregated schools, race riots, and lynchings. As the specter of the ''yellow peril'' was raised with the arrival of each new immigrant group, a series of exclusionary laws were passed prohibiting the immigration of the Chinese in 1882; of the Japanese, Koreans, and other Asians in 1924; and of the Filipinos in 1934. The culmination of this ''yellow peril'' movement was perhaps reached during World War II when over 110,000 West-coast Japanese, mostly American-born citizens, were imprisoned by the U.S. government in concentration camps.

While discrimination against APA groups persisted into the postwar era, the more overt forms prevalent during the prewar period were now less frequently encountered, and American attitudes toward APAs gradually improved. In 1965, the passage of a more equitable law (66 Stat. 197), which amended the immigration provisions of the McCarran-Walter Act of 1952, finally lifted the discriminatory immigration restrictions imposed by previous legislation. Partly as a result of this law, the rate of immigration from Asia, particularly from Hong Kong, Taiwan, Korea, and the Philippines, increased enormously. In fact, much of the several-fold increase in the Chinese, Filipino, and Korean populations in the United States since 1965 may be attributed to this recent immigration. More recently, since the withdrawal of the United States from Vietnam in 1975, nearly half a million Indochinese refugees have entered the country.

As may be discerned from the papers, the adaptation of the more recent Asian immigrants has varied, depending to some degree on their educational levels and previous socioeconomic circumstances. A large number of them have crowded into the inner-city Asian ghettoes of San Francisco, Los Angeles, New York, and other major cities, often living under conditions of abject poverty. Many others, however, have gone into small businesses and appear to be doing reasonably well. Still others, particularly those with high levels of education from the more affluent classes, have been relatively successful in various professional fields.

While a number of papers in this series cite the usual "push-pull" factors* in explaining the immigration from Asia, there has emerged, in recent years, a more sophisticated theory of causation based on the so-called "world-system" model.[1] According to this theory, the "push" and "pull" factors are not independent of each other, but are closely inter-related through the world economic system which evolved from a European-centered world economy in the sixteenth century. Those who subscribe to this theory view the economic expansionism of the western nations and their intrusion into Asia to seek new markets as the driving force behind the creation of the "push-pull" factors that have led over the past 130 years to the immigration from Asia.[2]

DEMOGRAPHIC CHARACTERISTICS

As stated, there has been a phenomenal growth in the APA population since the last census. The latest figures from the 1980 U.S. Census show the increases for the various APA groups.[3] (See following page.)

As these figures show, the Chinese are now the most populous APA group, followed by the Filipinos. Both groups have overtaken the Japanese, who were the largest APA group for the past several decades. With an increase of over 400 percent, the Koreans are by far the fastest growing APA group. The 1980 census also counted sizeable numbers of Pacific Islanders, mainly Hawaiians, Samoans and Guamanians. As a result of these increases, APAs now constitute about 1.5 percent of the total U.S. population. Since the APA population growth has been primarily due to the large influx of immigrants from Asia during the past decade and, to a lesser extent, to an increase in migration from the U.S. Trust Territories of Samoa

---

*"Push" factors are those that influenced the immigrants to leave their countries of origin, e.g., adverse economic conditions, famine, natural disasters, etc. "Pull" factors are those that attracted the immigrants to this country, e.g., relatives, availability of jobs, recruiters, etc.

and Guam, APAs who are foreign-born now outnumber those who are American-born.

Geographically, over 50 percent of the APAs still reside in the 3 Pacific-coast states and Hawaii. Increasing numbers are settling in other parts of the country, however, such as the Northeastern and Middle Atlantic states, where almost 30 percent of the APA population now reside.

Ethnic Group	Population*	Percent Increase 1970 to 1980
Chinese	806,027	85.3
Filipino	774,640	125.8
Japanese	700,747	18.5
Asian Indian	361,544	n.a.
Korean	354,529	412.8
Vietnamese	261,544	n.a.
Hawaiian	167,253	n.a.
Samoan	42,050	n.a.
Guamanian	32,132	n.a.
Total	3,500,466	128

*Since these figures did not become available until after some of the papers in this series had already been written, there may be some disparities between these figures and the estimated figures provided in some of the papers. It should also be noted that, as of this writing, specific population characteristics for individual ethnic groups, taken from the 1980 U.S. census, are unavailable.

The most recent data available on the enrollment of APA students in public elementary and secondary schools (K–12) are those collected in the 1978 survey of the U.S. Office of Civil Rights, which produced the following statistics:[4]

1. Out of a total enrollment of 41,836,257 students in the fall of 1978, 593,597, or 1.4 percent, were APAs.
2. Of these 593,597 APA students, 86,012, or 14.5 percent were limited- or non-English speaking. Fifty-four percent of these limited- or non-English speaking students were receiving English as a second language (ESL) or bilingual education services.
3. In the 1977–78 school year, 34,372 APA students graduated from high school.

At the college level, data collected by the National Center for Education Statistics in the fall of 1978 showed that 238,382 APA students were enrolled in institutions of higher education. They constituted 2.1 percent of the total enrollment in institutions of higher education. Of these 238,382 APA students, 181,463 were undergraduates, and the remainder were in professional schools, graduate students, or unclassified.[5]

Although statistics on the socioeconomic status of APAs are still not available from the 1980 census, they will undoubtedly reinforce the impressions created by the results of the 1970 census. These earlier data showed that APAs were among the most highly educated ethnic groups in the country and that their median family income exceeded that of White families. Due to such glowing socioeconomic indicators, APAs have been hailed by many as the "model minority" who, through hard work, patience, and perseverance, have overcome the adversities of racial discrimination and achieved success in American society.[6]

From even a cursory reading of the papers in this series, however, it should be readily apparent that the "model minority" image of APAs is inaccurate, misleading, and a gross overgeneralization. While it is true that many APAs have attained some measure of success, the fact is that there is still a far larger proportion of APAs who are poor than there is in the general population.

As pointed out in the papers by Chan and Tsang and Macaranas, many of the poverty-level APAs are recent Chinese and Filipino immigrants who have low levels of education and who do not speak English. Most of them end up living in the Chinatowns and Manilatowns, which, despite tourists' impressions to the contrary, are often the most impoverished areas of the cities in which they are located. Similar circumstances are being faced by many of the Indochinese refugees. Thuy notes in his paper that the second wave of Indochinese refugees, including the so-called "boat people" who are less educated and poorer than their predecessors, are having a difficult time subsisting in this country.

Pacific Islanders also do not fit the stereotype of the "model minority." Bell cites statistics showing that a disproportionate percentage of Hawaiians have incomes below the poverty level and are dependent on welfare. Although they are not covered in this series of papers, other Pacific Islanders, such as the Samoans and Guamanians, are experiencing similar hardships and facing problems very much like those of other economically disadvantaged minority groups.[7]

Moreover, the "model minority" stereotype is problematic even in the case of the more educated middle-class APAs to whom it is most often applied. When the income figures for APAs are adjusted for such demographic variables as education, age, geographic location, and hours per week worked, it is found that they are earning considerably less than their

White counterparts.[8] As most of the authors point out in their papers, APAs are typically underemployed in lower-echelon positions that are not commensurate with their education, age, and experience. This disparity is largely attributed to the persistence of racial discrimination, which today is far more subtle and, therefore, often more difficult to combat than the overt forms experienced by APAs in the past. Thus, none of the authors appear to accept the thesis that APAs constitute a "model minority" and, indeed, most of them seem to believe that APAs continue to be victims of racial discrimination, albeit more covert in form.*

Many APAs take strong exception to the "model minority" thesis for at least 2 reasons. First, this thesis has frequently been used against other minorities who have been admonished to follow the "shining example" set by APAs and to pull themselves up on their own without depending on government aid. It has, thereby, been used in an attempt to discredit the protests and demands of these groups for social justice and has created tension and competition between these other minorities and the APA groups. Second, it has served to perpetuate the pernicious myth that the APA communities take care of their own and face no serious social problems. The wide acceptance of this myth as fact has encouraged official neglect of the very real problems faced by many APAs on the pretext that they have no problems—and it has made it difficult for the APA communities to obtain assistance for much needed social programs.[9]

EDUCATIONAL PROBLEMS, NEEDS, AND PROGRAMS

Until recently, to even suggest that serious educational problems exist for APAs would have seemed to border on the absurd to many people, especially educators. APA students almost universally have been viewed as industrious, conscientious, and well-behaved high achievers, whose educational attainments, as we have discussed, have been widely acclaimed. As this series of papers makes amply clear, however, such a view is superficial at best and has contributed to widespread misconceptions that have impeded efforts to identify and meet the educational needs of APAs.

The following areas of concern have been delineated in order to summarize the educational problems, needs, and programs discussed by the various authors: (1) bilingual education, (2) bicultural/multicultural

---

*Recently, however, there has been a disturbing increase in the number of racial incidences of violence and vandalism against APAs and other ethnic groups. These overt acts of racism have been attributed to such White-supremacist organizations as the Ku Klux Klan and the American Nazi Party, which appear to be experiencing a resurgence nationwide.

education, (3) adult education, (4) higher education, and (5) parental involvement in education. The discussions of the authors in each of these areas have been summarized and, in some cases where elaboration is warranted, supplementary comments have been added.

Bilingual Education

Over 50 percent of the current population of APAs are recent immigrants, and they encompass many ethnic and national groups, as well as numerous linguistic groups. Many of these recent arrivals are non-English or limited-English speaking and face formidable language and cultural barriers in all spheres of life. The lack of English competency is especially debilitating for limited or non-English speaking (K–12) APA students (constituting at least 14.5 percent of the total APA student population)—it creates serious and often dysfunctional family/school discontinuities, alienates many of these students from pursuing their education, and may be the partial cause for increasing rates of school dropouts and juvenile delinquency among APA youth. Furthermore, lack of English competency severely limits students' employment opportunities and discourages them from venturing outside of the inner-city ghettoes.

As most of the authors indicate, bilingual education programs are, consequently, among the most pressing of the educational needs of APA students. In her paper, Yoshiwara mentions that 452 bilingual programs for APAs have been identified in various parts of the country. Yet, despite these numbers, current programs for APAs appear to be underfinanced in comparison to those for other non-English speaking groups. Due to the lack of resources, many programs appear to be fragmented and uncoordinated, and much more research is needed to determine what are the most appropriate and effective methods and materials for bilingual education. Large numbers of non-English speaking APA students, moreover, are still not being served because of the lack of qualified bilingual teachers and inadequate curriculum materials.

Bicultural/Multicultural Education

Due to the "Anglo-centric" orientation of most American schools, the curriculum usually omits or badly distorts the experiences and contributions of APAs. When information is presented, it is usually meager, superficial, or condescending, and often perpetuates timeworn stereotypes. And, as Chan and Tsang, Kim, and Bell all indicate, teachers are often insensitive to the special problems, needs, and unique learning characteristics of APA students, particularly of those who are recent immigrants.

Many teachers stereotype APA students as quiet, hard-working, and docile, which tends to reinforce conformity and stifle creativity. APA students, therefore, frequently do not develop the ability to assert and express themselves verbally and are channeled in disproportionate numbers into the technical/scientific fields. As a consequence, many APA students undergo traumatic family/school discontinuities, suffer from low self-esteem, are overly conforming, and have their academic and social development narrowly circumscribed.

To remedy these problems, a number of the authors propose programs in bicultural/multicultural education. Such programs require major changes in school curricula and teaching practices.[10] Speaking generally, they must be designed to provide multiple learning environments that match the academic and social needs of students from a variety of cultural backgrounds. While Kim, Yoshiwara, and Bell each describe in more detail what forms such programs may take, suffice to say that apart from a few isolated programs, such as the Kamehameha Early Education Program (KEEP) in Hawaii, bicultural/multicultural programs involving APA students have not been widely or effectively implemented.

Adult Education

While this area of education is explicitly identified as a concern by only one of the authors, a number of the essays indicate that serious problems are being faced by adults who are recent immigrants and are non-English speaking. Most must seek gainful employment immediately upon their arrival, yet, at the same time, they are in urgent need of gaining competency in English and in learning a new vocation. However, they have neither the time nor the money to take regular English classes or enroll in job training programs. Under such circumstances, they often find themselves trapped in low-paying, dead-end, and menial jobs.

All of these problems are exacerbated for the young adults in their late teens and early 20s who have dropped out of school. Because they speak little or no English, have no high school diploma and no job experience, their prospects of finding a decent job are practically nil, and large numbers of them are unemployed. Many of them end up joining the street gangs which have formed in recent years in several APA communities and have been increasingly engaged in crime and acts of violence.

In order to meet the different needs of these groups, a variety of well-conceived, innovative programs are needed, which will integrate English language and vocational training with culturally-sensitive approaches to job placement and family counseling.

Higher Education

College enrollment data indicate that large numbers of APAs can be expected to go on to institutions of higher education.[11] Yet, they face a multitude of problems in this area. It appears that most APAs will continue to be channeled into or gravitate toward the technical/scientific disciplines and develop their potentialities within a relatively narrow range of options. While Yoshiwara notes that Asian-American Studies programs have been established on a number of campuses, not nearly enough programs and courses are available to meet the social, psychological, and academic needs of all APA students.

In recent years, increasing numbers of APA students from low-income and/or recent-immigrant families have been recruited for college through special programs that provide them with financial aid. Unfortunately, most of them are ill-prepared for college and often do not receive sufficient tutorial and remedial assistance once they are on campus, and, consequently, many of them drop out after a semester or two.

One other problem concerns the difficulties being encountered by APAs who are pursuing or wish to pursue academic careers in higher education. Despite affirmative action, many of them are finding it difficult to gain access to available faculty positions. It should also be noted that American-born APAs are still grossly underrepresented on the faculties of most colleges and universities, and they are out-numbered 10 to 1 by foreign-born APAs.[12] Moreover, studies have shown that APA faculty are paid substantially below both their White and Black colleagues, despite the fact that their records of academic achievement are usually superior.[13]

A wide variety of approaches are needed to address these problems. Pre- and in-college career counseling programs should be developed to assist APA students in exploring and preparing themselves for a wider range of career options. More programs, such as Asian-American Studies, bilingual tutoring, and cross-cultural psychological counseling, should be offered to meet the social, psychological, and academic needs of APA college students. Finally, affirmative action for APAs must be pursued more vigorously to ameliorate serious existing inequities.

Parental Involvement in Education

As Chan and Tsang, Kim, and Bell indicate in their papers, APA parents are both concerned and involved with their children's education. However, because of the respect they have traditionally accorded to educators, APA parents are often reluctant to intervene in the education of their children even when they may be dissatisfied. This reluctance is often compounded by the insensitivity many teachers exhibit toward the special problems and needs of APA students.

APA parents are also discouraged from becoming involved in the education of their children by certain structural barriers that often exist in schools. Since both parents work in an unusually high proportion of APA families, they often find it difficult to attend parent/teacher conferences and PTA meetings. Furthermore, given their past unpleasant encounters with the institutions of the larger society, many of them mistrust and are intimidated by the large, impersonal bureaucracies of most modern school systems.[14]

To overcome these problems, educators must become more knowledgeable and sensitive to the special problems and needs of APA students and to the nature and functioning of APA families. Incentives should be given to teachers and administrators for placing greater emphasis on family/school relationships and on increasing parental involvement in the schools. School administrators should also be encouraged to experiment with ways of removing structural barriers between the schools and the family.

CONCLUSION

Some final comments about the papers and on the future prospects for the education of APAs should be made.

The essays discussing the Chinese, Filipinos, Indochinese, Koreans, and Japanese are primarily concerned with the experiences of these APA groups on the U.S. mainland. They do not, for the most part, deal with the experiences of these groups in Hawaii, where about 17 percent of the APA population resides. Although there are many parallels in these experiences, there are also significant differences. Conversely, Bell's paper covers only Hawaiians in Hawaii, but not those on the U.S. mainland. Moreover, other Pacific Islanders, such as the Samoans and Guamanians, whose experiences are quite different from that of the Hawaiians, are not treated in any of the papers.

It should also be noted that there are other authorities whose perspectives differ sharply from those of some of the authors of this series of essays. For example, a number of earlier writers tended to promote the image of APAs as a ''model minority''; whereas none of the present authors appears to subscribe to that viewpoint. On the other hand, there are other writers who present more radical perspectives that place much more emphasis on the position of APAs as an oppressed, exploited minority group.

Such differing perspectives are, of course, not surprising and unavoidable when one deals with anything as complex and subjective as the human experience.

As for the future prospects for the education of APAs, most of the authors may be characterized as being cautiously optimistic about these prospects. Given their relatively small numbers, APAs have always held a rather tenuous position in American society. In the past, the American public's perception of APAs has shifted abruptly with changes in the sociopolitical climate. Nevertheless, while they see many problems to overcome in the years ahead, most of the authors appear to believe that APAs will continue to make progress in the field of education. It is hoped that this series of papers will contribute to that progress by providing useful information to educators which will help them advance the education of Asian-Pacific Americans.

REFERENCES

1. Terence K. Hopkins and Immanuel Wallerstein, "Patterns of Development of the Modern World-System," *Review* (Fall 1977): 111–45; Alejandro Portes, "Migration and Underdevelopment," *Politics and Society* 8 (1978): 1–48; and Immanuel Wallerstein, *The Modern World System: Capitalist Agriculture and the Origin of the European World-Economy in the Sixteenth Century* (New York: Academic Press, 1974).

2. Hagen Koo and Eui-Young Yu, "Korean Immigration to the United States: Its Demographic Pattern and Social Implications for Both Societies," in *Papers of The East-West Population Institute No. 74* (Honolulu, HI: East-West Center, August 1981), pp. 1–31; Paul Takagi, "The New Asian Immigration and the Development of Racial Communities in the United States" (paper presented at the annual meeting of the American Sociological Association, Boston, August 29, 1979).

3. U.S. Department of Commerce, Bureau of the Census, *Race of the Population by States: 1980. 1980 Census of Population* (Washington, DC: U.S. Government Printing Office, July 1981), PC 80-S1-3.

4. U.S. Office of Civil Rights, *State, Regional and National Summaries of Data from the 1978 Civil Rights Survey of Elementary and Secondary Schools* (Alexandria, VA: Killalea Associates, Inc., 1980).

5. U.S. Department of Education, National Center for Education Statistics, *Fall Enrollment in Higher Education, 1978* (Washington, DC, 1980).

6. "Success Story: Outwhiting the Whites," *Newsweek* (June 21, 1971): 24–25; William Peterson, "Chinese and Japanese Americans," in *Essays and Data on American Ethnic Groups,* edited by Thomas Sowell (Washington, DC: Urban Institute, 1978), pp 65–106; and Sandra G. Boodman, "Korean-Americans: Pursuing Economic Success," *Washington Post,* 13 July 1978, p. 1.

7. Faye U. Munoz, "Pacific Islanders: Life Patterns in a New Land," in *Asian Americans: Social and Psychological Perspectives,* vol. 2, edited by Russell Endo, Stanley Sue, and Nathaniel N. Wagner (Palo Alto, CA: Science and Behavior Books, 1980), pp. 141–154.

8. Ki-Taek Chun, "The Myth of Asian American Success and Its Educational Ramifications," *IRCD Bulletin* 15 (1 and 2) (1980): 1–12; Bob H. Suzuki, "Education and the Socialization of Asian Americans: A Revisionist Analysis of the 'Model Minority' Thesis," *Amerasia Journal* 4 (2) (1977): 23–52.

9. E.H. Kim, "The Myth of Asian American Success," *Asian American Review* 2 (1975): 122–49; Tom Owan, "Asian Americans: A Case of Benighted Neglect" (paper presented at the National Conference of Social Welfare, San Francisco, May 13, 1975).

10. Bob H. Suzuki, "Multicultural Education: What's It All About?" *Integrated Education Journal* 17 (January–April 1979): 43–50.

11. U.S. Department of Education, National Center for Education Statistics, *Fall Enrollment in Higher Education, 1978* (Washington, DC, 1980).

12. Dorothy M. Gilford and Joan Snyder, *Women and Minority Ph.D.'s in the 1970's: A Data Book* (Washington, DC: National Academy of Sciences, 1977).

13. Thomas Sowell, *Affirmative Action Reconsidered* (Washington, DC: American Enterprise Institute, 1975).

14. Bob H. Suzuki, "The Asian-American Family," in *Parenting in a Multicultural Society*, edited by Mario D. Fantini and Rene Cardenas (New York: Longman, Inc., 1980).

Shattering Myths: Japanese-American Educational Issues

by Florence M. Yoshiwara

INTRODUCTION

The historical experiences of Japanese Americans are both similar to and different from other Asian-American groups. Like other Asians, their history has been marked by severe social, economic, and political racism. Their uniqueness, though, stems from their tragic and dramatic internment in concentration camps during World War II. Some 120,000 persons of Japanese ancestry, two-thirds of whom were United States citizens by birth, were interned without due process of law.

Twenty years after this trauma, however, Japanese Americans began to be depicted as "the successful minority." Success was defined as being acculturated, assimilated, and financially successful. They were proclaimed as having higher levels of educational attainment and median family income than other identifiable groups. This view served to disguise a number of major social and economic problems that continued to face the group.

In 1970, Japanese Americans were the largest Asian-American group, numbering 591,290. Over the past 10 years, however, their growth has been considerably less than other Asian groups because of the lower rate of immigration from a comparatively economically and politically stable Japan. The 1980 census ranks Japanese Americans as third in population behind Chinese and Filipino Americans.

This discussion will provide a historical overview of the Japanese Americans, as well as a demographic profile. It will also critique the myth of "the successful minority" and analyze major educational issues. The conclusion forecasts immediate and future needs of Japanese Americans in education.

HISTORICAL OVERVIEW

The history of the Japanese in America has always been directly related to the changing relationships between the United States and Japan. These relations have had serious implications on the social, economic, and political treatment of Japanese Americans.

From the early 1800s, the United States sought to penetrate long-isolated Japan. In 1853, after 2 unsuccessful attempts, Commodore Matthew C. Perry forced his way into Japan.[1] An ensuing revolution 14 years later toppled the Tokugawa Shogunate, and reestablished emperor rule under Emperor Meiji.[2] Meiji then dedicated Japan to speedy industrialization and militarization to meet the challenge of joining the world family of nations.[3]

The Japanese were not allowed to emigrate freely until 1885. Although isolated groups had come to California and Hawaii as early as 1867 as laborers and students, it was not until an agreement to ensure equal treatment was signed that Japanese were allowed to emigrate to the United States.[4] Japan was aware of the unequal treatment imposed on Asians both in Asia and in the United States.

The Japanese emigrated to the United States to seek greater opportunities: industrialization and militarization in Japan had led to high taxes, military conscription, and political turmoil, which many young men sought to escape.[5] In the United States, they worked at the lowest paying jobs in agriculture, the railroad, as domestics in homes, in gardens, in small service businesses, and in industry.

By July 1894, Japan had embarked upon its first foreign war—against China—in a dispute over the domination of Korea.[6] Again in China, in 1905, Japan battled Russia over Port Arthur.[7] Japan won both wars, and the world took notice of the first victory of a non-White over a White nation. These events had direct impact upon the Japanese Americans. First, President Theodore Roosevelt became involved as the mediator between Japan and Russia, mainly to preserve a balance of power in that part of the world.[8] Second, when San Francisco attempted to segregate Japanese students along with Chinese students in 1906, both Japanese officials and Roosevelt became embroiled in the settlement.[9] Japanese parents were insulted at this attempt to segregate their children. When they were ineffective in bringing about a settlement locally, they went to Washington to protest directly to the Japanese ambassador. To Roosevelt, who was eyeing increased trade with Japan, it was an embarrassment. He pressured to resolve the issue, and at the same time sought to restrict immigration of Japanese labor. The Gentlemen's Agreement of 1907–1908 initiated by Japan, served to settle the disagreement.[10]

Following the exclusion of the Chinese from America in 1882 (by the Chinese Exclusion Act), it was popular for politicians, labor unions, and the press to blame every social and economic ill on the Japanese. As the Japanese sought to elevate their economic status through land and business ownership, anti-Japanese racism increased and led to added segregation in schools, housing, and employment.[11] Worst of all, the alien Japanese were deemed "ineligible for citizenship" by law (*Ozawa v. United States*, November 13, 1922), and through this ruling, racist legislators passed laws which prohibited land ownership.[12] When this did not deter the Japanese, they were also prohibited from leasing land.[13]

Without citizenship, the Japanese were helpless to combat the events that were designed to dehumanize them and keep them in the cheap labor market. In 1924, the federal government passed an immigration law (Immigration Exclusion Act) which excluded the Japanese from entering the United States.[14] In 1885 they had been encouraged to come; only 39 years later, the Japanese were declared undesirable and excluded from further immigration.

From the beginning, the Japanese established families and organized communities. The American-born children, the Nisei, became the hope of the Issei, the foreign-born Japanese. For the Nisei and their parents, education was seen as the best means of "earning acceptibility" and financial success. Issei parents made great sacrifices to provide education and college degrees for their Nisei children.[15] But even a degree with honors failed to impress employers. During the 1930s, Nisei graduates could only find work as grocery clerks, family fruit stand operators, gardeners, or domestics.[16] Their plight was no improvement over the racist treatment which plagued their foreign-born parents.[17]

As the Nisei matured, they began to organize around their common concerns of discrimination. This resulted in the founding of the Japanese American Citizens League (JACL) in 1928. Although it had a small membership before the war, the JACL now has approximately 30,000 members.[18]

All Japanese Americans who were of age on December 7, 1941 can recall with horror the day when Japan attacked Pearl Harbor, and war broke out. Everyone feared going to war, but for the Japanese Americans, because of their past history, war with Japan had an even more ominous prospect.[19] The Issei (who were never allowed to become citizens) were now classified as enemy aliens. During the first few days after Pearl Harbor, many Issei community leaders were jailed and removed, leaving unprotected and anxious families.[20]

On February 19, 1942, President Franklin D. Roosevelt issued Executive Order 9066 which authorized the removal of all persons of Japanese ancestry, aliens and citizens alike, from the West Coast.[21] By May 1942, 120,000 persons were living in concentration camps away from the West Coast. Two-thirds of those were American citizens, interned without due process of law.

Japanese Americans brought case after case to court to challenge the wartime removal and internment. Through the painfully slow legal process, 4 cases reached the Supreme Court.[22] Three cases ended in judgements against the Japanese Americans. In late 1944, the fourth case brought to the Supreme Court by the Japanese Americans was settled in their favor and the camps began to be closed in 1945. Thus, Japanese Americans endured 4 years of life behind barbed wires knowing that they were unjustly imprisoned.[23] The 3 cases which justified the removal and internment of Japanese Americans are still being challenged through the "Redress and Reparations Campaign" currently being waged by the JACL and other organizations.[24]

During World War II, many Japanese Americans sought to "prove" their loyalty to America by volunteering for the armed services. From the concentration camps and from Hawaii the men formed the famed 442nd Infantry Battalion and 100th Battalion which served in North Africa, Italy, and France. Together they sustained the heaviest losses in the history of the U.S. Army and became the most highly decorated units in the U.S. Army.[25] In addition, the Nisei also served in the Military Intelligence Service in the Pacific War against Japan. They intercepted enemy messages, interrogated prisoners, and translated documents of the Japanese enemy.[26]

After World War II, Japanese Americans spent long years struggling to recover from the vast financial losses of their internment. They also fought vigorously for the removal of over 400 anti-Japanese laws, which still existed at both the state and national levels. With JACL at the helm, Japanese Americans overturned alien land laws, discriminatory immigration quotas, antimiscegenation laws, and secured naturalization privileges for alien Japanese.[27]

In recent years, Japanese Americans have been able to seize opportunities for advancement into many different fields. Their visibility is apparent in some areas of employment; while this does not indicate a resolution of all of their issues, it does indicate that Japanese Americans have become as heterogeneous as any group of Americans.

DEMOGRAPHIC CHARACTERISTICS

The demographic characteristics of Japanese Americans have been directly determined by patterns of immigration: the immigration restrictions of 1908 and the exclusion of 1924. Emigration from Japan began officially in 1885, but the Japanese did not emigrate in large numbers until 1900, which was the first year the total reached 10,000.[28] After 1908, there was a dramatic drop because of the restrictions imposed by the Gentlemen's Agreement. The 1930 census reported 138,834 Japanese in the U.S. (excluding Hawaii).[29] Until 1940, the population was almost totally confined to Hawaii and the West Coast.

In some respects, the wartime internment served to geographically displace the Japanese-American population. For example, in 1940 there were 462 Japanese Americans in Illinois; in 1950, for the first postwar census, the population had grown to 11,646. Since then, Illinois has remained as one of the top 5 Japanese-American population centers.[30]

The 1980 Census reported the total population of Japanese Americans in the United States to be 700,747 or 0.3 percent of the total population.[31] This represented an 18.5 percent growth from 591,290 in 1970, which also represented 0.3 percent of the total U.S. population.[32] A comparison of the 5 states with the highest Japanese-American populations in 1970 and 1980 shows very little shifting.[33]

	1970	1980	1970–1980 Percent of growth	Percent of total population
Hawaii	217,175	239,618	10.3	24.8
California	213,277	261,817	22.8	1.1
Washington	20,188	26,369	29.7	0.6
New York	19,794	24,524	20.5	0.1
Illinois	17,645	18,550	7.2	0.2

Although Japanese Americans were the largest Asian group in America for many decades, the 1980 census now ranks Japanese Americans number 3 in total population: Chinese Americans now rank first with a population of 806,027, and Filipino Americans rank second with 774,640.[34] Most Japanese Americans (80 percent) still reside on the West Coast and Hawaii. (In 1970, 81 percent resided in the West.)[35]

The 1970 census reported that 89.1 percent of the Japanese Americans were urban dwellers.[36] Research by Montero reveals that in his sampling in 1967 "only 4 percent of the Nisei sample live in predominately Japanese-

American neighborhoods . . . the majority (58 percent) live in non-Japanese neighborhoods.''[37] This represents a dramatic shift from their early history of life in Japanese American ghettoes.[38]

In 1976, the percentage of foreign-born Japanese Americans was 25 percent, which is in sharp contrast to the percentage of foreign-born among Chinese Americans (66 percent), Korean Americans (80 percent), Filipino Americans (66 percent), and Vietnamese Americans (95 percent or more).[39] These statistics have implications for educational needs of Japanese-American students. Additionally, 40 percent of the foreign-born Japanese lived in Japanese speaking households and 14 percent usually spoke the Japanese language.

The distribution of school-aged persons based upon the 1970 census was as follows:[40]

Elementary aged	99,778
Secondary aged	50,694
College aged	45,251

The median school years completed for Japanese Americans in 1970 were 12.4 years, and 67.4 percent were high school graduates.[41] The number of median school years completed for White Americans was 12.1. In 1970, there were regional differences in percentage of high school graduates with Illinois (77.5 percent) as the highest and Hawaii (60.3 percent) as the lowest. Only 26.3 percent of those 65 and over were high school graduates. The highest percentage of high school graduates were those who were 20–24 years old in 1970. Urban Japanese Americans tended to have a higher percentage of high school graduates (93.6 percent male and 93.8 percent female) compared to rural residents (89.0 percent male and 85.9 percent female). [42]

The short period of large-scale immigration of Japanese led to the formation of distinct generations of Japanese Americans. The Issei or first generation came to the United States between 1885 and 1924 when immigration was first allowed. From that time and roughly until World War II, the second generation or Nisei appeared. From the postwar period came the Sansei, or third generation Japanese Americans. Because of antimiscegenation laws and strictly followed codes of ethics among the Japanese, there was a low percentage of outmarriages among Issei and Nisei. But the Sansei generation has experienced a rising percentage of outmarriages. Outmarriages increased from a low of 2 percent in 1924 to 49 percent in 1972 in Los Angeles County. In 1972, the rate was 44 percent for males and 56 percent for females in Los Angeles County.[43]

In summary, Japanese Americans are presently the third largest in population of Asian-American groups. They have fewer foreign-born, tend to live integrated communities, and are basically urban dwellers. They have a high level of educational attainment. As we discuss other features of the Japanese-American community, we will discover that many of these statistics are actually deceiving and provide us with a very limited understanding of the group.

THE MYTH OF THE SUCCESSFUL MINORITY

During the turbulent 60s when minorities were clamoring for equality in all areas of life, writers began to point their fingers at the Japanese Americans as the minority that "made it" despite overwhelming odds. This view emerged only 20 years after the Japanese Americans had been released, discouraged and penniless, from the concentration camps of World War II. They were praised variously as the "model minority" and the "successful minority."

Writers argued that since the "bootstrap theory" had worked for Japanese Americans, why could not it work for Blacks, Chicanos, and others? William Petersen in a well-quoted article declared "By any criterion of good citizenship that we choose, the Japanese Americans are better off than any group in our society including native born whites."[44] In a 1971 Newsweek article, Petersen's point of view was reinforced with quotes from Harry Kitano who stated "Scratch a Japanese American and you will find a Wasp. . . . Common measures of success find the Japanese on the 'right' side of the ledger."[45] In 1969, journalist Bill Hosokawa remarked, "One by one the barriers vanished for the Japanese Americans—legal barriers, social barriers, barriers that blocked the way to job opportunities . . . Nisei were astonished and delighted to find themselves being wooed by employers."[46] More recently (1980) Wilson and Hosokawa have written that the success of Japanese Americans "was a remarkable achievement made possible by [their] exemplary conduct . . . during the war. . . ."[47] They concluded their historical survey with a glowing report of the postwar success of the Japanese Americans.[48] The evidence suggests that the myth of success is well entrenched.

To explore this myth further, let us look at the figures for the median income for Japanese-American families which, in 1970, was $12,515, compared to the total U.S. median income of $9,590.[49] And, 33 percent of the male Japanese Americans were involved in professional, technical, managerial, and administrative fields, compared to 25 percent of the total male work force.[50]

The "successful model" begins to crumble, however, by examining the data closely. For instance, the median family income figures do not take 2 important factors into consideration. First, a Japanese-American family usually has 2 or 3 wage earners in a single household, which tends to inflate the median family income figure. Second, the majority (80 percent) of Japanese Americans reside in West Coast states, which are established high cost-of-living regions.

A report by the U.S. Commission of Civil Rights demonstrates that, when comparable educational levels and salaries are matched, a significant discrepancy in the "success theory" and a different view of median income statistics become apparent.[51] In a table which demonstrates the percentage of high school graduates who are employed in occupations which require less than a high school diploma, we consistently see a higher percentage of Japanese Americans. In 1976, 44.4 percent of White Americans were working in jobs for which they were overqualified, while 48.8 percent of Japanese Americans were overqualified for their jobs.[52] In another table which indicates the percentage of persons with at least one year of college who are employed in occupations that typically require less education, the White percentage was 44.7 percent, while for Japanese Americans it was 49.4 percent.[53] Furthermore, when we examine another indicator which demonstrates median earnings of those with 4 or more years of college, the White median earnings were set at $15,165, while for Japanese Americans they were $14,253.[54]

These data demonstrate the persistence of discrimination in employment against Japanese Americans. Despite the high level of education achieved by the Japanese Americans, there is obviously no equality in jobs as seen by income figures.

The plight of the elderly Japanese American is even more shocking. In 1970, there were 47,169 (8.01 percent) Japanese Americans who were 65 years and over; 17.4 percent of these elderly Japanese were classified at the poverty level in California, where a major portion of the Japanese reside.[55] Because of discrimination in employment and the financial losses stemming from the internment of 1942–1945, these older Japanese Americans were excluded from jobs or opportunities to earn pensions. Most Issei were self-employed or employed in low-paying jobs that did not provide for retirement. Therefore, many elderly Japanese Americans are now faced with those problems which accompany poverty, such as inadequate housing, nutrition, and health services, along with the additional burden of being non-English speaking.

Dr. K. Patrick Okura in his address to the U.S. Commission on Civil Rights declared, ''There's a widespread belief that Asian and Pacific Americans do not suffer the discrimination and disadvantages associated with other minority groups. The stereotyping of Asian-Pacific Americans as a success model among minority groups by virtue of hard work, education, thrift, and initiatives, has lulled the general public into an attitude of what we call benign neglect to the extent that Asian-American concerns are secondary to the problems of other minority groups.''[56]

Most importantly, statistical data do not begin to tell the complete story about a people. Data cannot describe the heterogeneous nature of the Japanese Americans; they can only provide averages, which tell us very little. The successful minority myth is highly simplistic and biased.[57]

EDUCATION AND THE JAPANESE AMERICAN

For some 80 years, Japanese-American students have been the subject of numerous studies. Most studies in the past have indicated that Japanese-American students are hard working, high achieving, tend to be nonverbal, and select professions in science and math.[58] These stereotypes will be examined, along with additional educational issues which relate to the historical experiences of Japanese Americans.

Because it directly affects the self-image of Japanese-American children entering school, the most important educational issue concerns combating sterotypes and myths, which range from Japanese Americans being labeled foreign and culturally non-WASP, to their being assumed to be quiet, nonverbal, and high achievers. These stereotypes have implications for curricula, teacher-student relations, and career counseling. Related to this issue is the rationale and need for bilingual/bicultural programs for Japanese Americans.

The historical experience of Japanese Americans also includes many important issues which have relevance for classrooms at every level, including civil rights, the use of propaganda, redress and reparations, and the contributions made by Japanese Americans to the growth and development of the United States.

Myths, Stereotypes, and Multicultural Education

The federal government began efforts 15 years ago to promote cultural pluralism in schools to reflect the reality of our society. The concept of cultural pluralism implies that social-cultural distinctions must be recognized in our society. This is good and healthy and should be fostered. The study of social-cultural distinctions will lead to increased understanding of behavioral patterns and develop positive self-images for those who do not conform to White middle-class standards.

In another vein, Carlos E. Cortes in speaking of the power of the media declares "The media—television, motion pictures, magazines, newspapers, and radio—serve as some of the most powerful, relentless educators within the societal curriculum."[59] Eugene F. Wong attests to the racist nature of the media as it relates to Asians in the United States.[60] So even before the Japanese-American child enters school, others have formed impressions of him/her through the media.

It is a fact that a blue-eyed child is hardly ever questioned about the land of his/her birth, but even a third-generation Japanese-American child is frequently asked, "Where were you born?" or "When did you come from Japan?" The inability to accept the Japanese American as American becomes a form of rejection.

In 1968, during the height of the desegration programs, Japanese-American educators began to communicate their concerns about the lack of materials on Japanese Americans for use in multicultural programs. Groups organized to call attention to this need. They pointed out that much of the material written about Japanese Americans was inaccurate. For instance, Noel Leathers in *The Japanese in America*, wrote that the United States was the "adopted country" of the Japanese Americans.[61] If you were born a citizen of the U.S., your country would not be "adopted." Leathers also wrote that the evacuation was "the safest procedure in view of the wartime excitement. . . ."[62] More seriously, none of these books described how the Japanese Americans fought against discrimination. They were depicted solely as passive victims. For example, Ritter, Ritter, and Spector in *Our Oriental America* mentioned the $36,000,000 paid to Japanese Americans after the war, but they did not mention that the Japanese Americans launched, financed, and fought the battle with the government which resulted in the payment.[63] Nor did they mention that this amount was less than 10 percent of the estimated losses incurred by the Japanese Americans.

One of the groups which organized in the late 1960s was the Japanese American Curriculum Project (JACP), a nonprofit educational organization in San Mateo, California. The JACP began a drive to develop more accurate Japanese-American curricula and materials written from the Japanese-American point of view. After their initial projects, the JACP began to disseminate materials and expand their concern to Asian-American materials in general. All of their offerings are examined for accuracy and usefulness for the classroom and home. Presently, JACP offers over 300 different materials on Asian Americans, ranging from preschool to university levels. A descriptive catalog may be obtained by sending $1.00 to JACP, Inc., 414 E. 3rd Ave., San Mateo, CA 94401.

Good materials applied sensitively can go a long way toward eliminating stereotypes. Two good guides which educators can use to judge materials are "The Portrayal of Asian Americans in Children's Books," *Council of Interracial Books for Children Bulletin*, 7 (2 & 3) (1976) and *The Asian Image in the United States*, New York: Asian Americans for Fair Media, 1974. Both may be obtained from JACP.

Always being described as quiet, hard-working, nonverbal, and high-achieving places unfair burdens on Japanese-American students. When teachers encourage this type of behavior, they reward students for remaining stereotypic. Teachers need to encourage verbal skills and consciously select Japanese-American students to engage in discussions, debates, and presentations. It is very important to create an atmosphere in which Japanese-American students can feel comfortable enough to pursue their own paths in society. To ensure this kind of environment, Japanese Americans in selected areas have organized special programs.

Bilingual and Bicultural Programs

Demographic information on Japanese Americans indicates that 25 percent are foreign-born in contrast to much higher percentages for Chinese, Korean and other Asian-American groups. Therefore, bilingual/bicultural education has different implications for them. This does not mean that there is a lesser need, but instead different needs.

The *Directory of Asian and Pacific American Bilingual Programs in the United States* lists a total of 452 bilingual programs for 1980; of these, only 28 programs either contain a Japanese-English element, section, or separate program.[64] This is 6 percent of the total. Since Japanese account for approximately 20 percent of the Asian- and Pacific-American population, 6 percent appears to be a very small share of bilingual programs.

The San Francisco Unified School District offers a program which is an example of a full-time bilingual/bicultural Japanese/English program, funded through Title VII. This program came about through the concerted efforts of concerned parents of the district. In 1969, the San Francisco Japanese Speaking Society of America presented a request to the San Francisco Unified School District for a Japanese bilingual/bicultural program. Their request was denied on the basis that such a program did not command the support of the Japanese-American community. The JSSA then joined forces with the Japanese Community Services to explore educational issues of all Japanese-American students. In 1973, the Board of

Education approved a Japanese bilingual/bicultural program for kindergarten through second grade. From that beginning, the present program now has 348 students at 3 school sites and 9 classroom teachers for kindergarten through seventh grade. All regular subjects required by the district are taught through this program. They include reading, math, social studies, language arts, science, physical education, art, music, and multicultural studies. Also included in the curriculum are Japanese language and culture, i.e., music, arts, festivals, games, foods, and family and community life. Upon visiting the classroom, one can immediately sense a warm supportive environment for Japanese-American students where they can learn about a more positive self-image and learn to speak and write English. The pictures on the wall, the curriculum materials, and the teachers all support self-identity as a Japanese American. This is an environment in which students learn about things which have a direct relationship to them as individuals, learn a language which will help them communicate with their grandparents, and learn activities and skills which will fill them with special pride in being Japanese Americans. Here the recent immigrant child can learn English in a friendly, supportive environment and may even be perceived as an expert in skills that his/her American-born friends are just learning.

Because many Japanese Americans have begun to recognize the effects of racism on the self-image of their children, they have taken steps to prevent this kind of psychological damage. One step has been to organize a number of special private programs for Japanese-American children which help them develop more positive self-images by learning their own culture through history, crafts, language, arts, and foods. Held during the summer months, examples of these programs include the Suzume No Gakko, in San Jose, California and the Jan Ken Po Gakko in Sacramento.

The Concentration Camps and World War II: Their Ramifications for Education

The concentration camp experience of Japanese Americans during World War II stands out as one of the most glaring examples of the abrogation of civil rights of United States citizens. Roger Daniels states ''it is possible to argue that the massive violations of civil liberties of one group, the West Coast Japanese, was an ominous prefiguration of the future in which an increasingly powerful federal bureaucracy would exercise more and more surveillance and potential control over groups and individuals seemed, in one way or another, to be deviant.''[65] Michi Weglyn in her book, *Years of Infamy,* writes ''. . . I hope this uniquely American story will serve as a reminder to all those who cherish their liberties of the very fragility of their rights against the exploding passions of their more numerous fellow citizens, and as a warning that they who say that it can never happen again are probably wrong."[66]

The concentration camp story should be included in every classroom discussion on civil liberties, along with examples of violations against Blacks, Native Americans, and other groups. Civil liberties cannot be taught without a warning to students that their constant vigilance is the only safeguard for *all* citizens.[67]

Social studies curricula usually include the concept of propaganda, its use, and ramifications. Yet rather than focus on examples from American history, they tend to use the Nazi example, which is foreign. The unjust removal of the Japanese Americans would never have been possible without a carefully executed plan of justification through the news media of the time. The newspapers and radios were filled with innuendos built upon rumors which people accepted as fact. A typical example from that period is as follows:

> Information from Pearl Harbor, now well authenticated, reveals that when officers and men got the sudden call to report to their stations they were impeded and seriously delayed in many instances by farm implements, jallopies, and any other obstacle at hand, placed in the street during the night.[68]

Although Japanese Americans were not mentioned by name, the strong inference was there. This statement has since been proven to be completely false, but the impact that such a barrage of similar statements had at the time can be imagined. Japanese Americans, alien and citizen alike, were always referred to as "Japs," a very derogatory and inflammatory term. Newspapers and radios frequently used the term until Japanese Americans put a stop to it.

To this day, these rumors and half-truths are still believed by the masses rather than the facts as researched and written later. It is a demonstration of the impact of propaganda and how easy it is to play upon racism to create an air of panic. With this artificially created diversion, those with evil intent were free to plunder innocent victims.

An amazing World War II saga is that of the Japanese Americans who volunteered out of concentration camps and Hawaii for the 100th Infantry Battalion and the 442nd Regimental Combat Team. Fighting on the battlefields of North Africa, Italy, and France with "Go for Broke" as their motto, these units became among the most highly decorated in the U.S. Army, yet they suffered a tragically high casualty rate.[69] And, the intriguing story of the Japanese Americans in the Military Intelligence Service in the South Pacific tells of a possibly more heroic group of men. Working in an arena in which they could be and often were mistaken for the Japanese enemy, they were the important secret weapon of the U.S. Army, and were instrumental in turning the tide of war much earlier than anticipated by military experts of that time.[70]

In 1980, Congress established the Commission on Wartime Relocation and Internment of Civilians to reinvestigate the evacuation period and to make recommendations for appropriate redress. During 1981, the Commission held hearings throughout the United States to receive testimonies from Japanese Americans and other concerned persons. The hearings began in Washington D.C. during July, 1981. Japanese Americans have also set out to challenge the Supreme Court decisions which justified their incarceration without due process of law. This drive towards achieving justice for Japanese Americans through monetary reparations will result in the strengthening of the civil rights of all Americans. Three Japanese-American organizations which have been directly involved in the redress and reparations campaign are (1) The National Committee for Redress of the Japanese American Citizens League, 1765 Sutter Street, San Francisco, CA 94115, (415) 921-5225; (2) National Coalition for Reparation and Redress, 244 South San Pedro, Room 406, Los Angeles, CA 90012; and (3) National Council for Japanese American Redress, 925 West Diversey Parkway, Chicago, IL 60614. You can write to any of these organizations to receive materials concerning redress for use in the classroom. It is anticipated that this issue will be before the public for many years before it is resolved.

Contributions of Japanese Americans

There are numerous other issues which justify the American education system's including Japanese Americans in the study of the growth and development of the United States. Japanese Americans, for instance, played a major role in the development of California as an agricultural state.[71] There are many aspects of the Japanese-American culture which can be included in the study of arts, crafts, and literature. Nationally known personalities in the arts include Isamu Noguchi, sculptor; Ruth Asawa, sculptor; Minoru Yamasaki, architect; Chiura Obata, artist; Mine Okubo, artist; and Sono Osato, dancer.[72] Crafts include origami (the art of paper folding), sumi-e (the art of brush painting), and calligraphy (the art of writing with the brush). Outstanding Japanese-American writers include Toshio Mori, John Okada, Milton Murayama, Monica Sone, Yoshiko Uchida, Janice Mirikitani, Lawson Inada, Mitsuye Yamada, Hisaye

Yamamoto, Wakako Yamauchi, and Momoko Iko.[73] Hiroshi Kashiwagi writes short plays about the Japanese Americans. These are but a few examples of the wealth of literary artists among Japanese Americans.

The musical group, Hiroshima, has composed numerous songs, performed many concerts, and displayed their unique blending of Japanese instruments and American sounds.[74] There are also a number of performing Taiko Drum groups which carry on the tradition of celebrating festivals and festive occasions with their performances. In a number of urban areas there are organized Asian-American theatre groups like Los Angeles' East-West Players who perform plays about the Asian-American experience.

Exploring the Japanese-American community can be an interesting project. It can be a meaningful sequel to classroom history studies, providing contributions of a small but vigorously heterogeneous minority group.

ASIAN-AMERICAN STUDIES PROGRAMS

Asian-American studies at the university level were born during the turbulent 60s. Contrary to most predictions, Asian-American studies programs have existed for over 10 years and continue to generate student interest, despite unfriendly and uncooperative campus administrations.

From their experimental beginnings, Asian-American studies programs have grown to support intellectual inquiries into the "political, economic, and historical forces affecting Asian Americans."[75] The continued existence of these programs depends upon students and faculty who are willing to wage the never ending battle against the cutbacks in budgets and staffing which are intended to decrease the programs.

Northern California remains the stronghold for Asian-American studies because 2 of the largest programs in terms of student enrollment are located there. In 1978, both San Francisco State University and the University of California at Berkeley estimated their student enrollments to be 1500.[76] Other programs are located on the West Coast and in other parts of the country.

The University of California at Los Angeles (UCLA) has perhaps the most well-known Asian-American studies program because of its ambitious publishing projects. It issues *Amerasia Journal*, which has become the most respected journal in the field. In addition, it has published a number of other books and materials used by students throughout the United States.[77] UCLA also houses the Japanese-American Research Project Collection, the most extensive archival collection in the country dealing with Japanese Americans.

As Nakanishi and Leong have stated in *Amerasia Journal,*

The goals of Asian American Studies programs remain diverse. For some programs, the goals of Asian American Studies remain consistent with its founding goals—to provide students with an alternative educational perspective, to provide them with involvement in the decision making process and planning of programs, and to provide a progressive framework for serving Asian American communities.[78]

The recent influx of Asian immigrants poses a new challenge for Asian-American studies. Their perceptions about themselves as Asians are quite different from second- and third-generation Asian Americans; Asian immigrant students have been raised in a different environment than the founders of Asian-American studies programs (who tend to be third generation).

The rise in foreign-born Asians and the rising interracial marriages among Asians will necessarily become important factors in the future development of Asian-American studies. There has been little discussion about how these factors will change Asian-American studies, but the challenge of change is an unavoidable certainty.

CONCLUSION

The history of the Japanese in America has been filled with many forms of racism. It is a history which is little known and much misunderstood, from the concentration camp experience to the myths which tend to declare that Japanese Americans are successful and without problems. This paper has attempted to dispute those myths, while also demonstrating the diversity of the group.

When levels of education and corresponding income are compared with White Americans, we find that Japanese Americans receive a lower salary at every educational level. When we examine the poverty level among elderly Japanese Americans, we find an alarmingly high level of poverty. These data are not compatible with success. There is still discrimination in employment which prevents Japanese Americans from earning salaries which are commensurate with their educational levels. The poverty of the elderly stems from long years of job discrimination and the devastations of the concentration camps which left them with little or no retirement benefits.

In looking at the concentration camp experience of the Japanese Americans, there still remains a great deal of misunderstanding, based upon the propaganda that inundated the news media during 1941–45. This single action by the United States government had a serious effect upon all Japanese Americans. They are still struggling to correct the violations of civil rights which occurred during their evacuation and internment. In the classroom, this issue has many implications for the study of civil rights and the uses of propaganda.

For Japanese Americans, "A more practical solution that many Japanese Americans have chosen to follow during the stringent 1970s is the capture of enhanced self-esteem through a reinvigorated wedding of their Japanese selves with their American heritage. Their goal is not to fuse themselves, but to relate to both traditions in varying degrees.[79]

If we recognize that Japanese Americans have been the victims of one of the worst episodes of racism against Asians in America and see that Japanese Americans are receiving only 6 percent of the federal monies allotted to Asian-American bilingual/bicultural programs, then we would need to conclude that there are some serious disparities in educational funding where Japanese Americans are concerned. In the case of the Japanese Americans, bilingual/bicultural education is necessary to overcome the racist heritage under which they still suffer.

While bilingual/bicultural programs are needed at the primary and intermediate levels, Asian-American studies programs are needed at the secondary and university levels. It is clear that Japanese Americans' educational needs are numerous and justifiable. The time has come for funding agencies to recognize that Japanese-American education needs must be met to resolve concerns which have many other implications than just the mollification of a people. There is much to be learned from Japanese-American history and culture through the present Japanese-American community.

JAPANESE/ENGLISH BILINGUAL PROGRAMS IN THE UNITED STATES

Anchorage School District, Pouch 6-614, Anchorage, AK 99502
   (907) 333-9561
West Lake School, 80 Fieldcrest Dr., Daly City, CA 94014
William Land School, 2020 12th St., Sacramento, CA 95818
Einstein Junior High School, 5050 Conrad Ave., San Diego, CA 92117
Madison High School, 4833 Doliva Dr., San Diego, CA 92117
Anza School, 40 Vega St., San Francisco, CA 94115   (415) 922-0200
Morning Star School, 1715 Octavia St., San Francisco, CA 94109
   (415) 921-4436

Presidio Middle School, 450 30th Ave., San Francisco, CA 94121
    (415) 753-9696
Sherman School, 1651 Union St., San Francisco, CA 94123
    (415) 776-5500
Hawaii Bilingual/Bicultural Education Project, 233 S. Vineyard St.,
    Honolulu, HI 96813   (808) 548-3493
Champaign Central High School, 610 W. University, Champaign, IL 61820
Ray Harte School, 5641 S. Kimbark Ave., Chicago, IL 60625
Einstein School, 345 W. Walnut, Des Plaines, IL 60016
High Ridge Knolls Center, 588 S. Dara James, Des Plaines, IL 60016
Mark Hopkins, 231 S. Shadywood Ln., Elk Grove, IL
Chute Middle School, 1400 Oakton, Evanston, IL 60202
Dewey School, 1551 Wesley Ave., Evanston, IL 60201
Eisenhower Junior High School, 800 W. Hassell Rd., Hoffman Estates,
    IL 60195
Sanborn School, 101 N. Oak St., Palatine, IL 60067
Plum Grove Junior High School, 2600 W. Plum Grove Rd., Rolling
    Meadows, IL 60067
Schaumburg School, 520 E. Schaumburg Rd., Schaumburg, IL 60194
Martin L. King School, 1008 W. Fairview, Urbana, IL 61801
Stevenson School, 1375 S. Wolf Rd., Wheeling, IL 60090
Louise E. McKenzie School, Central and Prairie, Wilmette, IL 60091
Eastchester School District, 580 White Plains Rd., Eastchester, NY 10707
Douglas School System, Box Elder, SD 57719
Laurelhurst School, 4530 46th Ave., N.E., Seattle, WA 98105
Tacoma Public Schools, #10, P.O. Box 1357, Tacoma, WA 98401

RESOURCES

Organizations

Asian American Studies Center, 3232 Campbell Hall, University of California, Los Angeles, CA 90024.
Developers and disseminators of university level journals and books.

Japanese American Citizens League, National Headquarters, 1765 Sutter
St., San Francisco, CA 94115, (415) 921-5225.
National organization for advocacy. Request free informational materials.

Japanese American Curriculum Project (JACP), Inc., 414 E. 3rd Ave., San
Mateo, CA 94401, (414) 343-9408.

Nonprofit educational organization which sells Asian-American books and materials. Catalog available upon request. Send $1.00

National Association for Asian and Pacific American Education, P.O. Box 367, San Mateo, CA 94401.
Issues copies of research papers related to Asian-American educational issues presented at their annual conferences. List available upon request.

Publications

Pacific Citizen, The National Publication of the Japanese American Citizens League, 244 S. San Pedro, Rm 506, Los Angeles, CA 90012. Published weekly.

Audiovisuals

Note: These resources are available for preview/purchase from JACP, Inc., 414 E. 3rd Ave., San Mateo, CA 94401.

JACP, Inc., *Prejudice in America: The Japanese Americans,* Stanford, CA, Multi Media Productions, 1971.
Secondary level; 4 filmstrips and cassettes on Japanese-American history.

JACP, Inc., *Japanese Americans: An Inside Look,* Stanford, CA, Multi Media Productions, 1974.
Elementary/secondary level; 2 filmstrips and cassette.

Visual Communications, *I Told You So,* Los Angeles, CA, 16mm black & white, 18 minutes.
A film about Lawson Inada, a well known Japanese-American poet.

Visual Communications, *Wataridori: Birds of Passage,* 16mm color, 37 minutes.
Covers the experience of the first generation Japanese in the United States.

REFERENCES

1. John K. Fairbanks, Edwin O. Reischauer, and Albert M. Craig, *East Asia Tradition* (Boston: Houghton Mifflin Co., 1973), pp. 486–87.
2. Mikiso Hane, *Japan, a Historical Survey* (New York: Scribner's Sons, 1972), pp. 245–62.
3. Hane, pp. 262–344.

4. Katharine Coman, *History of Contract Labor in the Hawaiian Islands* (New York: Macmillan Co., 1903; reprinted at New York: Arno Press, 1978), p. 42.

5. Yamato Ichihashi, *Japanese in the United States* (Stanford: Stanford University Press, 1932; reprinted at Arno Press: NY 1969), p. 1–15.

6. Fairbanks, et al., pp. 553–4.

7. Hane, op.cit. p. 367–75.

8. Charles E. Neu, *An Uncertain Friendship, Theodore Roosevelt and Japan, 1906–1909* (Cambridge: Harvard University Press, 1969), p. 8.

9. Frank F. Chuman, *The Bamboo People: The Law and Japanese Americans* (Del Mar, CA: Publishers, Inc., 1976), pp. 19–37.

10. Thomas Bailey, *Theodore Roosevelt and the Japanese American Crises* (Gloucester: Peter Smith, 1964).

11. Roger Daniels, *The Politics of Prejudice, the Anti-Japanese Movement in California and the Struggle for Japanese Exclusion* (New York: Atheneum, 1977).

12. Chuman, p. 70.

13. Chuman, pp. 73–89.

14. Chuman, pp. 98–103.

15. Robert W. O'Brien, *The College Nisei* (Palo Alto, CA: Pacific Books, 1949; reprinted at New York: Arno Press, 1978), pp. 6–7.

16. Bill Hosokawa, *Nisei, the Quiet Americans* (New York: William Morrow, 1969), p. 169.

17. Harry H. L. Kitano, *Japanese Americans, the Evolution of a Subculture*, 2d ed. (Englewood Cliffs, NJ: Prentice Hall: 1976), pp. 11–68.

18. Hosokawa, pp. 191–205.

19. Robert A. Wilson and Bill Hosokawa, *East to America, A History of the Japanese in the United States* (New York: William Morrow, 1980), pp. 188–201.

20. Jacobus tenBroek, Edward N. Barnhart, and Floyd W. Matson, *Prejudice, War and the Constitution, Causes and Consequences of the Evacuation of the Japanese Americans in World War II* (Berkeley, CA: University of California Press, 1954), p. 103.

21. Roger Daniels, *The Decision to Relocate Japanese Americans* (New York: J.B. Lippincott, 1975).

22. tenBroek, Barnhart, and Matson, pp. 211–23.

23. Michi Weglyn, *Years of Infamy; the Untold Story of America's Concentration Camps* (New York: William Morrow, 1976), p. 21.

24. Refer to JACL, Redress Campaign, 1765 Sutter St., San Francisco, CA 94115.

25. Chet Tanaka, *Go For Broke, A Pictorial History of the Japanese American 100th Infantry Battalion and the 442nd Regimental Combat Team* (San Francisco: Go For Broke, Inc., 1982).

26. Joseph D. Harrington, *Yankee Samurai, The Secret Role of Nisei in America's Pacific Victory* (Detroit, MI: Pettigrew Enterprises, 1979).

27. Chuman, pp. 309–45.

28. Yamato Ichihashi, *Japanese in the United States* (Stanford, CA: Stanford University Press, 1932; reprinted at New York: Arno Press, 1969), p. 66.

29. Ichihashi, p. 64.

30. Harry H.L. Kitano, *Japanese Americans: The Evolution of a Subculture*, 2d ed. (Englewood Cliffs, NJ: Prentice Hall, 1976, 2nd Ed.), p. 211.

31. U.S. Department of Commerce, Bureau of the Census, *1980 Census of Population Supplementary Reports, Race of the Population by States: 1980* (Washington, DC: U.S. Government Printing Office, July, 1981), p. 7.

32. U.S. Department of Commerce, *1980 Census* . . . , p. 13.

33. U.S. Department of Commerce, *1980 Census* . . . , p. 13.

34. U.S. Department of Commerce, *1980 Census* . . . , p. 13.

35. U.S. Department of Commerce, *1980 Census* . . . , p. 13.

36. United States Department of Commerce, *Japanese, Chinese and Filipinos in the United States, 1970 Census of Population,* (Washington, DC: U.S. Government Printing Office, July, 1973), p. 1.

37. Darrel Montero, *Japanese Americans: Changing Patterns of Ethnic Affiliation Over Three Generations* (Boulder, CO: Westview, 1980), p. 37.

38. B.S. Frank Miyamoto, *Social Solidarity Among the Japanese in Seattle* (Seattle, WA: University of Washington, 1981 reprint of 1939 monograph).

39. U.S. Department of Health, Education, and Welfare, Education Division, National Center for Education Statistics. "Birthplace and Language Characteristics of Persons of Chinese, Japanese, Korean, Filipino and Vietnamese Origin in the United States," *Bulletin* (May 21, 1979).

40. U.S. Department of Commerce, U.S. 1970 Census, p. 9. [Note: Most 1980 U.S. Census figures for specific ethnic populations are not yet available.]

41. U.S. Department of Commerce . . . 1970 Census . . . , p. 17.

42. U.S. Department of Commerce . . . 1970 Census . . . , p. 17.

43. Harry H.L. Kitano and Akemi Kikumura, "The Japanese American Family," in *Asian Americans: Social and Psychological Perspectives,* ed. by Russell Endo, Stanley Sue and Nathaniel N. Wagner (Palo Alto, CA: Science and Behavior Books, 1980).

44. William Petersen, "Success Story, Japanese American Style," *New York Times Magazine* (9 January, 1966): 20.

45. ———, "Success Story: Outwhiting the Whites," *Newsweek* (June 21, 1971): 24–25.

46. Bill Hosokawa, *Nisei: The Quiet American* (New York: William Morrow 1969), p. 473.

47. Robert A. Wilson and Bill Hosokawa, *East to America: History of the Japanese in the United States* (New York: William Morrow, 1980), p. 286.

48. Wilson and Hosokawa, p. 257–85; and Hosokawa, p. 473–488.

49. U.S. Department of Commerce, Bureau of the Census, *Japanese, Chinese, and Filipinos in the United States, 1970 Census of Population,* Washington, DC: U.S. Government Printing Office, July 1973, p. 42, Table 9.

50. U.S. Department of Commerce, *Japanese, Chinese, and Filipinos in the United States,* p. 13–39.

51. U.S. Commission on Civil Rights, *Social Indicators of Equality for Minorities and Women* (Washington, DC: U.S. Government Printing Office, 1978), pp. 18–21.

52. U.S. Commission on Civil Rights, p. 18, Table 2.5.

53. U.S. Commission on Civil Rights, p. 20, Table 2.6.

54. U.S. Commission on Civil Rights, p. 24, Table 2.7.

55. U.S. Department of Commerce, *Japanese, Chinese and Filipinos in the United States.*

56. *U.S. Commission on Civil Rights, Civil Rights Issues of Asian and Pacific Americans: Myths and Realities,* (Washington, DC: U.S. Government Printing Office, May 1979), p. 669.

57. A very helpful resource paper is by Ki-Taek Chun, Henry A. Gordon, Esther Walters and Cathy H. Somers, *Success of Asian Americans: Fact or Fiction?,* U.S. Commission on Civil Rights (Washington, DC: U.S. Government Printing Office, September, 1980).

58. Harry H.L. Kitano, *Japanese Americans: the Evolution of a Subculture* (Englewood Cliffs, NJ: Prentice Hall) 1976, p. 196; United States Department of Commerce, *Japanese, Chinese and Filipinos in the United States, 1970 Census of Population* (Washington, DC: U.S. Government Printing Office, July, 1973), pp. 98–99.

59. Carlos E. Cortes, "The Role of Media in Multicultural Education," *Journal of the School of Education, Indiana University,* 56 (1) (Winter 1980): 39.

60. Eugene Franklin Wong, *On Visual Media Racism, Asians in the American Motion Pictures* (New York: Arno Press, 1978).

61. Noel L. Leathers, *The Japanese in America* (Minneapolis, MN: Learner Publications, 1967), p. 40.

62. Leathers, p. 47.

63. Ed Ritter, Helen Ritter, and Stanley Spector, *Our Oriental America* (San Francisco, CA: McGraw-Hill, 1965), p. 70.

64. Asian American Bilingual Center et al, *Directory of Asian and Pacific American Bilingual Programs in the United States* (Berkeley, CA: Asian American Bilingual Center, June 1980).

65. Roger Daniels, *The Decision to Relocate the Japanese Americans* (New York: J.B. Lippincott Company, 1975), p. 3.

66. Weglyn, p. 22.

67. For a complete listing of classroom resources, refer to the current catalogue of JACP, Inc., Box 367, San Mateo, CA 94401.

68. *Wartime Hysteria: the Role of the Press,* (San Mateo, CA: JACP, Inc., 1971), p. 3.

69. Chet Tanaka, *Go For Broke, A Pictorial History of the Japanese American 100th Infantry Battalion and the 442nd Regimental Combat Team* (San Francisco: Go For Broke, Inc., 1982).

70. Joseph D. Harrington, *Yankee Samurai* (Hallandale, FL: Pettigrew Enterprises, Inc., 1979).

71. Masakazu, Iwata, *Planted in Good Soil, Issei Contributions to United States Agriculture* (Honolulu, HI: University of Hawaii Press, 1982).

72. Sam Hunter, *Isamu Noguchi* (New York: Abbeville Press, 1965); Tobi Tobias, *Isamu Noguchi, the Life of a Sculptor* (New York: Crowell, 1974); Minoru Yamasaki, *A Life in Architecture* (Tokyo: Weatherhill, 1979); Chiura Obata, *Through Japan with Brush and Ink* (Rutland, VT: Tuttle, 1969); Mine Okubo, *Citizen 13660* (New York: Arno Press, 1969); and Sono Osato, *Distant Dances* (New York: Knopf, 1980).

73. Toshio Mori, *The Chauvinist* (Los Angeles: UCLA, 1979); John Okada, *No No Boy* (reprinted at Seattle, WA: University of Washington Press, 1957); Milton Murayama, *All I Ask For Is My Body* (San Francisco: Supa Press, 1979); Monica Sone, *Nisei Daughter* (reprinted at Seattle, WA: University of Washington Press, 1953); Yoshiko Uchida is a prolific writer of children's books—See JACP brochure for listing of available books; Janice Mirikitani, *Awake in the River* (San Francisco: Isthmus Press, 1978); Lawson Inada, *Before the War* (New York: William Morrow, 1971); and Mitsuye Yamada, *Camp Notes and Other Poems* (San Lorenzo, CA: Shameless Hussy Press, 1976).

74. Hiroshima has produced two records: *Hiroshima*, Arista Records and *Hiroshima Odori*, Arista Records. There are additional recordings by Asian-American composers and performers.

75. Don T. Nakanishi and Russell Leong, "Toward the Second Decade, a National Survey of Asian American Studies Programs," *Amerasia Journal* 5 (1) (1978): 1–2.

76. Nakanishi and Leong, p. 9.

77. For further information write to Asian American Studies Center, 3232 Campbell Hall, University of California at Los Angeles, Los Angeles, CA 90024.

78. Nakanishi and Leong, p. 18.

79. Gene N. Levine and Colbert Rhodes, The *Japanese American Community: A Three-Generation Study* (New York: Praeger, 1981), p. 153.

SELECTED BIBLIOGRAPHY

Bailey, Thomas A. *Theodore Roosevelt and the Japanese American Crises*. Gloucester, MA: Peter Smith, 1934.

Bosworth, Allan. *American Concentration Camps*. New York: W. W. Norton, 1967.

Chuman, Frank F. *The Bamboo People: The Law and Japanese Americans*. Del Mar, CA: Publishers Inc., 1976.

Chun, Ki-Taek. "The Myth of Asian American Success and Its Educational Ramifications." *IRCD Bulletin*, 14 (1 & 2) (Winter/Spring 1980).

Daniels, Roger. *Concentration Camps U.S.A.* New York: Holt, Rinehart and Winston, 1971.

———. *The Decision to Relocate the Japanese Americans*. Philadelphia, PA: Lippincott, 1975.

Hosokawa, Bill. *Nisei: The Quiet Americans*. New York: Morrow, 1969.

Ichihashi, Yamato. *Japanese in the United States*. New York: Arno Press, 1979.

Kashima, Tetsuden. *Buddhism in America: The Social Organization of an Ethnic Religious Institution*. Westport, CT: Greenwood Press, 1977.

Kitano, Harry. *Japanese Americans: The Evolution of a Subculture, 2nd ed.* Englewood Cliffs, NJ: Prentice Hall, 1974.

Montero, Darrel. *Japanese Americans: Changing Patterns of Ethnic Affiliation Over Three Generations*. Boulder, CO: Westview Press, 1980.

Petersen, William. *Japanese Americans: Oppression and Success*. New York: Random House, 1971.

tenBroek, Jacobus, Barnhart, E., and Matson, F. *Prejudice, War & the Constitution*. Berkeley, CA: University of California Press, 1954.

U.S. Commission on Civil Rights. *Civil Rights Issues of Asian and Pacific Americans: Myths and Realities*. (Washington, DC: U.S. Government Printing Office, 1979).

U.S. Department of Commerce. *1970 Census of Populations: Japanese, Chinese and Filipinos in the United States*. Washington, DC: U. S. Government Printing Office, 1973.

Weglyn, Michi N. *Years of Infamy: The Untold Story of America's Concentration Camps*. New York: Morrow, 1976.

Wilson, Robert A., and Hosokawa, Bill. *East to America: A History of the Japanese in the United States*. New York: Morrow, 1980.

Overview of the Educational Progress of Chinese Americans

by Kenyon S. Chan and Sau-Lim Tsang

Approximately 806,000 of the 3.5 million persons of Asian ancestry residing in the United States are of Chinese heritage, which makes this ethnic group the largest Asian group in the United States.[1] While statistically the Chinese are only .4 of 1 percent of the total U.S. population, they have been a prominent cultural and ethnic influence in the multicultural fabric of American life. Other Americans are often intrigued by the lifestyle, food, and rich cultural heritage displayed by their fellow Chinese inhabitants. Most persons living in or visiting cities such as San Francisco, Los Angeles, or New York have visited at one time or another the "Chinatown" in each of these places. Many non-Asians have become fond of Chinese cuisine and art. Behind these superficial appearances, however, lies a very complex and diverse ethnic group which defies easy description or understanding. The purpose of this essay is to present a brief sketch of the educational progress of the Chinese in America and to introduce the reader to the complexities and problems they face.

WHO ARE THE CHINESE IN AMERICA?

It is impossible to describe *the* Chinese Person in America. Persons of Chinese ancestry living in America range from recent immigrants to sixth-generation Chinese Americans. The Chinese were the first Asians to immigrate to the United States in large numbers. Their migration to the West Coast in the 1840s was encouraged by economic depression and social unrest in China and by overpopulation in certain provinces.[2] Californians initially welcomed the Chinese immigrants because they provided cheap labor during a period of high inflation brought on by the Gold Rush.[3] Chinese immigrants quickly filled domestic service jobs and were hired to help build the Transcontinential Railroad. As the labor market diminished, however, and as the Chinese began to enter into the gold fields, anti-Chinese sentiment emerged. American hostility towards the Chinese was well-formed by 1852 and continued through the 1860s and 70s during which time many Chinese were assaulted and killed by White mobs. The anti-Chinese movement culminated in passage of the Chinese Exclusion Act of 1882, which was made permanent in 1902 and not repealed until the beginning of World War II when China became an American ally.[4]

The Chinese population in the United States changed significantly after World War II. A comparison of 1960 and 1970 U.S. census data shows that the Chinese population in the United States grew by 84 percent. The majority of this increase was due to immigrants who came to the United States between 1965–1970 after the enactment of the Immigration and Naturalization Act of 1965. Still in effect, this act allows 20,000 immigrants per country into the United States. Coupled with the waves of post-Vietnam refugees, many of whom are ethnically Chinese, the 1980 census is likely to show an even sharper increase in the Chinese population in the United States. Because the Chinese population in the United States has grown significantly since 1965, research conducted before then must be viewed with some caution.

WHAT ARE THE DEMOGRAPHIC CHARACTERISTICS OF THE CHINESE IN AMERICA?

As of 1979, 34 pecent of the Chinese in America were American-born, and of the foreign-born Chinese, 79 percent originated from China.[5] It was not possible, however, to distinguish among those originating from the People's Republic of China, Taiwan, or Hong Kong. It was also not possible to ascertain which dialect of Chinese was spoken, although from available data it was known that 83 percent of the Chinese in the United States live in homes where Chinese was spoken. Half that number included families in which only Chinese was spoken; the remainder lived in bilingual homes or homes in which English was usually spoken.[6]

Although conflicting data exist,[7] the analysis by the U.S. Commission on Civil Rights in 1978 suggested that the Chinese in America had attained educational parity with majority group males. In 1976, 88 percent of Chinese men and 90 percent of Chinese women aged 20–24 had completed 12 or more years of school; 60 percent of Chinese males and 44 percent of Chinese females aged 25–29 had completed college. While the educational attainment of Chinese in America seemed comparable to the majority population, education-to-job equity was substantially less for the Chinese as compared to other groups. More than half of Chinese males and females with more than one year of college were overqualified for the jobs they held. Male Chinese college graduates earned 84 percent of what the majority culture male college graduates earned. Cabezas and Yee found in 1977 that, compared to their proportion of the population, Chinese were underrepresented in high-wage job categories (e.g., managerial/administrative) and overrepresented in blue collar or low-wage jobs (e.g., seamstress, food service, clerical, and cleaning).[8] Educational attainment is not necessarily the route to social or economic parity.

The median income for Chinese families in 1970 was $10,610, slightly better than the median family income for the total U.S. population ($9,950).* This statistic, often quoted as a sign of success, is misleading. The Chinese in America reside largely in urban areas, with nearly 60 percent living in San Francisco, Los Angeles, New York, or Honolulu. Since the majority of Chinese families live in urban settings, the median family income must reflect the higher cost of urban living. As an indication of the influence that living in concentrated urban settings has on the median income, it was found that the income for Chinese males in urban areas was considerably lower than it was for Whites, Blacks, or Hispanics in every metropolitan area except Los Angeles.[9]

In addition, the median family income figures may not be the best statistics to use for comparing income parity, because they do not account for differences in the number of persons living in a family. A better indicator of economic status is the median income per capita within a household. This statistic represents the average available income for each member of the household unit, taking into account differences in family size. The U.S. Commission on Civil Rights in 1978 reported that the median household income per capita for a Chinese family was 11 percent less than it was for a household headed by a majority culture male. Using household income per capita, Chinese were 1.89 times more likely to be living in poverty than families headed by majority culture males. For Chinese female-headed households, the statistics were even more bleak.

---

*Although 1980 U.S. Census figures for Chinese Americans are not yet available, 1980 census figures for Asian and Pacific Islanders show a median income figure of $22,075 for this group, as compared with the nationwide median of $19,908. 1980 census figures also show that high school education rates for Asian and Pacific Islander were 75 percent as opposed to 69 percent for Whites, 50 percent for Blacks, and 43 percent for Hispanics. The Asian figure however, is not broken down into the various ethnic groups. Ethnic groups are likely to vary considerably.

Chinese female-headed households had 59 percent less income than the majority culture male-headed families and were 2.11 times more likely to be living in poverty.[10]

Furthermore, a number of authors have pointed out that the Chinese family has a proportionately higher number of multiple wage earners in the family unit than the average American family.[11] In Chinese-headed households, more people are making less money than in majority group households.

It can be concluded that the Chinese in America are a largely urban group, comprised of both American-born and foreign-born persons who are fairly well-educated, overworked, and underpaid. A fuller critique of the myth of the Asian-American success story can be found in a cogent analysis by Chun. As he states, ''When examined closely, the image of Asian-American success dissolves helplessly, baring strands of past discrimination, sacrifice and overwork, preoccupation with survival, and disquieting feeling of lost identity.''[12]

CULTURAL CHARACTERISTICS

Several authors have described the general features of Chinese-American culture and its role in psychological development.[13] For example, Lee (1952) investigated the relationship between parent/child cultural conflicts and Chinese-American delinquency; Kung (1962) and Hsu (1971) described Chinese family and kinship patterns as characterized by obedience and cooperation.[13] Kriger and Kroes (1972) found Chinese mothers to be more restrictive in child rearing attitudes than Jewish and Protestant mothers.[14] Steward and Steward (1977) observed Anglo-Mexican, and Chinese-American mothers teaching their preschool-aged children a sorting and motor skills game. They found that Chinese-American mothers offered significantly less input than Anglo mothers but gave more enthusiastic, positive feedback than any other group.[15] The teaching style of Chinese mothers was also characterized by their specificity of instruction. Kim, in her 1978 analysis of Asian Americans in the Chicago area, found that Chinese families continued to rely on extended family ties and friends for assistance in child rearing.[16]

Although characterizations of stable personality traits of any population have not been successful, it should be noted that the Chinese have been characterized as generally obedient, conforming, punctual, and respectful of authority.[17] Teachers have often described Chinese children as quiet, well-behaved, and obedient.[18] Personality characterization may be based

largely on stereotypic perceptions of the population and lack an appreciation for the diversity of children in the Chinese-American community.
Observations of Chinese-American children at home and at school would
reveal many different personalities and find children who may be quiet in
one setting and gregarious and talkative in another setting.

LEARNING CHARACTERISTICS

Chinese students have been described by many as high achievers. A
review of the several studies comparing the academic achievement of
different ethnic groups shows that Chinese students have achieved at or
slightly higher than the national norm.[19] All these studies, however, derived
their results from data collected before or immediately after the passage of
the Immigration and Naturalization Act of 1965. As noted earlier, the
population has increased and diversified drastically since 1965, and the
characteristics and background of these new immigrants are different from
those already living in the U.S. Pre-1965 research is likely to provide
inaccurate indicators of the current achievement levels of Chinese-American students. With the influx of new immigrants, there is likely to be an
increase in the number of Chinese pupils who speak little or no English,
who are from low socioeconomic backgrounds, and who have diverse
experiences with formal education. These and other characteristics of new
immigrants are likely to present new challenges to American education.

In addition to demographic and experience differences, some researchers have suggested psychological differences between Chinese and
majority culture persons. Several studies have investigated different con-
structs of cognitive styles of Chinese students. Hsi and Lim (1977) re-
viewed these studies and concluded that, while Chinese students differed
from other comparison groups in various cognitive styles, the differences
were inconsistent and efforts to explain the differences were unsatisfactory.[20] If confirmed, however, differences in cognitive styles could
implicate differences in learning styles, as well as information processing.

Language-learning studies have reported that the reading and writing
styles of students whose first language is Chinese differed from those whose
first language was English.[21] Similarly, in mathematics, researchers have
found that Chinese immigrant students' understanding of mathematics
concepts differed from U.S. born students.[22]

The above studies provide a limited picture of the learning characteristics of Chinese students. In general, the results suggested that the learning
characteristics of Chinese students, especially immigrant students, differ

from U.S. students. However, little is known about how these different learning characteristics affect a Chinese student's school performance. Indeed, there are many learning styles, and, therefore, differences in learning characteristics may suggest a need for curricular flexibility rather than a need for remedial training or readjustment of culturally relevant learning styles. More research is necessary before a comprehensive profile of the learning characteristics of Chinese students can be developed and applied in classroom curricula and pedagogies.

THE CHINESE AND BILINGUAL EDUCATION

Bilingual education, sometimes called bilingual/bicultural education, can be broadly defined as instruction in both English and the students' home language. Depending on whom one asks, the goals of bilingual education vary but usually consist of one or more of the following: (1) to teach the content subjects in a language the students understand while they acquire English language proficiency, (2) to use culturally relevant curricula to facilitate learning and to increase students' self-concepts, and (3) to maintain the students' home languages and culture through classroom instruction. Envisioned as results of bilingual education are children who communicate competently in English and their home language and who operate successfully in both the mainstream society and in their home environment.[23]

A form of bilingual education in the Chinese community began in the nineteenth century when the early Chinese immigrants settled in the U.S. Because the few immigrants with families found that their children were not allowed into the public schools, private schools were organized. The curricula in these private schools consisted mainly of Chinese classics, and the language of instruction was Chinese. The schools' main goal was to inculcate into the children the traditional Chinese virtues and thus to develop Chinese scholars.

Later, when public schools started to accept Chinese students, most of the private Chinese schools changed their operational hours to the late afternoons or weekends. Chinese parents sent their children to the public schools to learn the English language and other subjects and, after the regular school hours, to private Chinese schools for the maintenance of the Chinese language and culture. Hence, there was an early form of bilingual education.

The "modern" Chinese bilingual education movement began in 1968 when federal funds were awarded to establish self-contained Chinese bilingual programs in 2 public schools, one in New York and one in San Francisco, for the limited English speaking (LES) and non-English speaking (NES) Chinese students. In the next several years, schools in several cities with high concentrations of Chinese, such as New York and Boston, also received funds to operate bilingual programs.

At approximately the same time—in 1970—Chinese parents brought the *Lau* v. *Nichols* (414 U.S. 565, 1974) suit against the San Francisco Unified School District, claiming that the schools were not providing equal educational opportunities to Chinese students, because they were instructed in a language they did not understand. The plaintiff asked for bilingual education as the remedy, and the case went to the U.S. Supreme Court. In 1974, the court ruled in favor of the plaintiff and mandated the San Francisco Board of Education rectify the problem by providing services to meet the special linguistic needs of Chinese students.[24]

The *Lau* v. *Nichols* ruling, though it did not specify any remedy, provided further momentum for bilingual education. Several states passed legislation mandating bilingual education for LES and NES students. The Title VII Bilingual Education Act of 1968 provided seed money for establishing demonstration bilingual programs and has produced a steady increase in bilingual education programs in the last decade.

Currently, bilingual education programs can be found in every city with a large Chinese population. To provide services to the school programs, a network was established under Title VII consisting of resource centers which provide direct services to schools requesting information or technical assistance, material development centers to develop bilingual curricula, and dissemination and assessment centers that publish bilingual curriculum materials and provide technical assistance in assessment to school districts. There is also a nationwide clearinghouse, the National Clearinghouse for Bilingual Education, which gathers and disseminates information related to bilingual education.[25]

The concept and implementation of bilingual education is not without criticism. Some argue that it is the duty of the LES or NES student to learn the English language and that the most effective way is to immerse the child in an all-English curriculum at school. Others believe that a culturally relevant (bilingual) curriculum promotes ethnocentrism in the students and prevents them from interacting with and integrating into mainstream society.

Maintenance of the home language and culture is the most controversial aspect of bilingual education. Some critics state that a home language other than English has no place in U.S. society, while others suggest that maintenance of a home language handicaps a child's English language acquisition. Many critics also believe that the teaching of Chinese in schools takes away instructional time for English as a second language, as well as other subject matters. Others state that, while they support the maintenance of home languages, it is the function of the Chinese language schools and not the federal government nor the public school system to support non-English instruction. Finally, there are those who fear that the maintenance of home language and culture will lead to separatism among the various ethnic groups in the United States.

Supporters of bilingual education counter their critics by suggesting that bilingual education does not inhibit the acquisition of English and, in fact, provides a far richer educational experience for non-English and English speaking children who enroll. They also argue that the maintenance of one's home language and culture is a basic right in this multicultural nation and strengthens, rather than weakens, the society. Bilingual/bicultural education is said to promote better academic achievement, better mental health, and better adaptation to adult life than monolingual education. Supporters of bilingual education point to educational systems around the world which promote rather than inhibit multiple language learning.

Many of the arguments for and against bilingual education are based largely on myths or emotions. While recent studies of bilingual education have indicated the relative success of the program, the sparse amount of research on bilingualism and bilingual education has not provided policymakers or educators with concrete data on the pros and cons of bilingual education. A wide spectrum of research—including the establishment of the National Center for Bilingual Research—is currently being supported by the National Institute of Education. These efforts will shed light on this controversial idea.

CONCLUSION

This brief overview of the educational progress of the Chinese in America has examined the complex characteristics of this ethnic group. In particular, Chinese children in American schools represent a diverse group of students, ranging from fifth- and sixth-generation American citizens to those who are recent immigrants. Chinese pupils vary in their approach to learning as well as in their degree of acculturation into the mainstream of American life. Chinese pupils also represent a diverse linguistic group, with some children who speak fluent English and no Chinese, and others who are limited or non-English Chinese speakers. In short, the Chinese in America represent a changing and complex ethnic group whose learning styles, motivation, aspirations, and accomplishments are not easy to stereotype and are not yet completely illuminated.

REFERENCES

1. U.S. Census Bureau, State Census Data Center, Population Research Unit, 1982.

2. V. Purcell, *The Chinese in Southeast Asia*, 2d ed. (London: Oxford University Press, 1965); D. W. Sue, "Ethnic Identity: The Impact of Two Cultures on the Psychological Development of Asians in America," in *Asian Americans: Psychological Perspectives*, by S. Sue and W. Wagner (Ben Lomond, CA: Science and Behavior Books, 1973), pp. 140–49.

3. H. H. L. Kitano, *Race Relations* (Englewood Cliffs, NJ: Prentice-Hall, 1974).

4. M. Miller, *The Unwelcomed Immigrants: The American Image of the Chinese, 1785–1882* (Berkeley, CA: University of California Press, 1969); A. Saxton, *The Indispensable Enemy: Labor and Anti-Chinese Movement in California* (Berkeley, CA: University of California Press, 1971); and D. W. Sue, pp. 140–49.

5. U.S. Department of Health, Education and Welfare, National Center for Education Statistics, "Birthplace and Language Characteristics of Persons of Chinese, Japanese, Korean, Filipino, and Vietnamese Origin in the United States, Spring 1976," *NCES Bulletin* (1979): 79–144.

6. U.S. Department of Health, Education and Welfare, National Center for Educational Statistics, pp. 79–144.

7. B. L. Kim, *The Asian-American: Changing Patterns, Changing Needs* (Urbana, IL: AKCS Publication Services, 1978).

8. A. Cabezas and H. Yee, *Discriminatory Employment of Asian Americans: Private Industry in San Francisco-Oakland SMSA* (San Francisco: ASIAN, Inc., 1977).

9. T. Owan, "Asian Americans: A Case of Benighted Neglect" (paper presented at the National Conference of Social Welfare, San Francisco, CA, May 1975) (ERIC document ED 159 154).

10. U.S. Commission on Civil Rights, *Social Indicators of Equality for Minorities and Women* (Washington, DC: U.S. Commission on Civil Rights, 1978).

11. Cabezas and Yee; K. T. Chun, "The Myth of Asian American Success and Its Educational Ramifications," *IRCD Bulletin* 15 (1 and 2) (1980): 1–12.

12. Chun, p. 9.

13. K.S. Chan, R. Takanishi, and M. Kitano, *An Inquiry into Asian American Preschool Children and Families in Los Angeles*, Working Papers in Asian American Studies, no. 6 (Los Angeles, CA: Asian American Studies Center, University of California at Los Angeles, 1975) (ERIC document ED 117 251); F. Hsu, *The Challenge of the American Dream: The Chinese in the United States* (Belmont, CA: Wadsworth Publishing, 1971); S.W. Kung, *Chinese in American Life* (Seattle, WA: University of Washington Press, 1962); R.H. Lee, "Delinquent, Neglected, and Dependent Chinese Boys and Girls of the San Francisco Bay Region," *Journal of Social Psychology* 36 (1952): 15–41; D.W. Sue, pp. 140–49; D.W. Sue and B.A. Kirk, "Psychological Characteristics of Chinese-American Students," *Journal of Counseling Psychology* 19 (1972): 471–78; and B.L. Sung, *Mountain of Gold* (New York: MacMillan, 1967). Reprinted as *Story of the Chinese in America* (New York: Collier Books, 1971).

14. S.F. Kriger and W.H. Kroes, "Child-Rearing Attitudes of Chinese, Jewish, and Protestant Mothers," *The Journal of Social Psychology* 86 (1972): 205–10.

15. M. Steward and D. Steward, "The Observation of Anglo-, Mexican-, and Chinese-American Mothers Teaching Their Young Sons," *Child Development* 44 (1973): 329–37.

16. B.L. Kim.

17. S. Sue, D.W. Sue, and D.W. Sue, "Asian Americans as a Minority Group," *American Psychologist* 30 (1975): 906–10; W. Mischel, "Toward a Cognitive Social Learning Reconceptualization of Personality," *Psychology Review* 80 (1973): 252–83.

18. R. Suzuki, "Education of the Asian-American Family" (paper presented for the Conference on Pacific and Asian American Families and HEW-Related Issues, Arlington, VA, March 1978).

19. M.E. Backman, "Patterns of Mental Abilities: Ethnic, Socioeconomic and Sex Differences," *American Educational Research Journal* 9 (1972): 1–12; G.S. Lesser, G. Fifer, and D.H. Clark, "Mental Abilities of Children from Different Social-Class and Cultural Groups," in *Monographs of Society for Research in Child Development* 30 (4) (1965); G.W. Mayeske et al., *A Study of the Achievement of Our Nation's Students* (Washington, DC: U.S. Government Printing Office, 1973); and S.S. Stodolsky and G. Lesser, "Learning Patterns in the Disadvantaged," *Harvard Educational Review* 37 (1967): 564–93.

20. V. Hsi and V. Lim, *A Summary of Selected Research Studies in Cognitive and Perceptual Variables* (Berkeley, CA: Asian-American Bilingual Center, 1977).

21. M. Chu-Chang and D.J. Loritz, "Phonological Encoding of Chinese Idiographs in Short Term Memory," *Language Learning* 27 (1977): 341–52; K.F. So, M.C. Potter, and R.F. Friedman, *Chinese Characters, English Words and Drawings: Naming and Understanding* (Unpublished manuscript, 1976); O. Tseng and W.S. Wong, "Speech Recording of Chinese Characters," *Journal of Experimental Psychology* 27 (1977): 621–30; and F.L. Wong, "Some Error Types in the Written English of Chinese Speakers" (paper presented at the CATESOL Bay Area Mini-Conference, 1979).

22. K.M. Ng and S.L. Tsang, "Mathematical Cognitive Structures of Chinese American, Euro-American, and Hong Kong Chinese Students" (paper presented at the American Educational Research Annual Conference, Boston, April 1980); S.L. Tsang, "The Effects of the Language Factor and the Cultural Content Factor of Mathematics Achievement Tests on Chinese and Chicano Students" (Unpublished Ph.D. diss., Stanford University, 1976).

23. F. Cordasco and G. Bernstein, *Bilingual Education in American Schools* (Detroit, MI: Gale Research Co., 1979); H. LaFontaine, B. Persky, and L. Golubchick, eds., *Bilingual Education* (Wayne, NJ: Avery Publishing Group, 1978).

24. *Lau* vs. *Nichols,* 414, U.S. 563, 1974; H. Teitelbaum and R.J. Hiller, *Bilingual Education Current Prospective Law* (Arlington, VA: Center for Applied Linguistics, 1977).

25. Information on the national support network for bilingual education can be obtained by calling the National Clearinghouse for Bilingual Education at 800-336-4560 (toll free) or by writing to 1300 Wilson Boulevard, Suite B2-11, Rosslyn, VA 22209.

The Future of Korean-American Children and Youth: Marginality, Biculturality, and the Role of the American Public School

by Bok-Lim C. Kim

Some years ago, my 5-year-old son came home from school, shortly after entering kindergarten in a predominantly White neighborhood, and asked, "What am I? Am I a Korean or an American?" Trying to be a good mother, I told him that he was a *Korean American*; he was born in the United States of Korean parents and had rich heritages from 2 cultures. This did not comfort my son, nor did he seem to feel enlightened by the knowledge of his bicultural background. Instead, he protested, "If I am a Korean, why can't I speak Korean like you do? And if I'm an American, how come I don't look like the American kids in my class?" He paused for a moment and then delivered the final blow: "Besides, they call me Chinese!"

He was not only bewildered and frustrated, but angry over his muddled identity as a Korean American. The Korean and American parts of him seemed to be opposite poles, and a Korean-American identity that would somehow unite them seemed hopelessly elusive. It did not make sense to him that I was urging him to be proud of his bicultural heritage when he clearly perceived that he was in some ways different from both his parents and his classmates.

My son is not alone in wondering about his bicultural identity as he moves back and forth between the rather different worlds of his school and his home. At present, there are an estimated 80,000 children of Korean ancestry in American schools. About 80 percent of them are immigrant children who came to the United States in the past decade.[1] It is probably too early to tell definitively what sort of adaptations they will ultimately make. Some will surely develop a rich bicultural identity, selecting and integrating the heritages and strengths of 2 cultures, while others will probably fall into a state of marginality, feeling that they belong to neither culture and hence have no cultural identity to call their own.

This paper will discuss various educational needs and issues of Korean-American children and youth within the context of the rapidly evolving Korean-American community in the United States. First, the immigration history and demographic characteristics of the Korean-American group will be presented, followed by a discussion of the educational needs and problems of Korean-American children as they relate to existing educational programs. Finally, parent and community attitudes toward and involvement in the education of these children will be explored, using data from a study conducted by the author.

DEMOGRAPHIC CHARACTERISTICS OF KOREAN AMERICANS

At present, approximately 420,000 Korean immigrants and native-born Korean Americans live in the United States, representing a vast increase over 1970, when the census reported a total of 70,510 Korean Americans.[2] With such growth, it is likely that the present population may be different in some ways from that counted in 1970. Survey data taken since then, however, and some other information taken from the 1970 census, allow us to make some generalizations about the Korean-American population that are pertinent to this discussion.[3]

Of the Korean Americans enumerated in 1970, only 44 percent (about 31,000) were of native birth; 60 percent of the American-born persons of Korean ancestry (about 18,600) were under 19 years of age. These persons presumably represent native-born children of immigrant parents. Likewise, survey research by Kim and others has found most Korean immigrants to be relatively young couples with young children.[4] This suggests that the Korean Americans as a group may be particularly susceptible to any sort of problem that may arise between immigrant parents and children—whether native- or nonnative-born—who are attending and being acculturated by American public schools.

Although the majority of the present Korean-American population are composed of fairly recent arrivals who benefitted from the 1965 Immigrant and Naturalization Act Amendment,[5] the first Korean immigrants came to the United States between 1903 and 1905. Spurred by political and socio-economic instability and encouraged by their government, some 7,226 Koreans (6,048 men, 637 women, and 541 children) emigrated to work on

Hawaiian plantations during those years. The immigrants were mostly poor farmers, and nearly half were converted Christians.[6] In 1905, the Korean government prohibited all further emigration upon learning of the harsh working conditions of Koreans in Hawaii. Consequently, only a limited number of "picture brides" were allowed to emigrate until the late 1920s.[7] A few Korean students and visitors who considered themselves political exiles also were admitted to the United States, from where they worked to free Korea from Japanese domination and to regain national independence. Upon the liberation of Korea by the allied forces after World War II, a sizable number of these former students and political exiles returned to Korea. Notable among the returnees was Sung Man Rhee, the first elected president of the Republic of Korea.

It was not until the late 50s that a significant number of Koreans immigrated to the United States. Because of the discriminatory U.S. Immigration and Nationality Law, the number of immigrants of Korean nationality was miniscule.[8] For instance, in 1950, only 10 were admitted as immigrants. By 1965, the quota had grown to 103 persons, but actual immigration in 1965 alone totalled 9,108 per year. Thus the vast majority of Koreans immigrating to the United States prior to 1965 were persons exempt from the quotas—"war orphans" or "war brides"—who came to the United States through adoption or marriage to American citizens. This form of immigration was a direct result of U.S. involvement in the Korean Conflict.

The annual number of immigrants to the United States from Korea has increased steadily and dramatically since the present immigration ceiling of 20,000 replaced the 103 quota limitation in 1968. In the past 3 years, the number of Korean immigrants, including both quota and nonquota persons, has averaged 31,000 per year. This heavy immigration is partially due to a situation common in many developing nations: the educational system has produced more educated and trained individuals than can be absorbed by the economic system.

Geographic Location

The 1980 census indicated that Korean Americans were more widely dispersed among all regions of the United States than any other Asian-American group. The largest number, 43.4 percent, lived in western states such as California and Hawaii; of the remainder, 19.2 percent lived in the northeastern states, 17.5 percent in the north central region, and 19.9 percent in the southern region.

The annual reports of the Immigration and Naturalization Service through 1977 suggest that this pattern of scattered settlement has continued, although there has been secondary migration into such large metropolitan areas as Los Angeles, Chicago, New York City, the District of Columbia, San Francisco, and Honolulu.

Sex and Age Distribution

The median age of Korean Americans in 1970 was 26 years, and slightly over one-third were 18 years and under. Of the total number of Korean immigrants (121,807) arriving between 1970 and 1975, more than half were between 20 and 30 years of age. Nationally, only 3 percent of the Korean group was made up of older persons.

Unlike other Asian-American groups, the sex ratio of Korean Americans has favored females during the last two and a half decades, primarily due to the immigration of young female children adopted transracially by American parents and young interracially married Korean women. While a trend toward a more balanced sex ratio is evident among the recent immigrants, there were still twice as many females as males admitted to the United States between 1970 and 1977. The imbalance is even more pronounced among immigrants in 2 age groups: of the children under age 5, 63 percent are females, and women represent 82 percent of the 20–29 age group.[9]

Educational Attainment

In 1970, more than one-third (36.3 percent) of the Korean Americans had completed 4 or more years of college education, compared to 11.3 percent of the total U.S. population. Fully 71 percent of Korean Americans had completed high school and fewer than 20 percent of the adult population had less than an eighth grade education. There is much collaborative statistical evidence from several studies which show even higher education achievement among recent immigrants.[10]

Employment, Income, and Household Size

The 1970 census statistics on employment and income characteristics of the Korean-American population are extremely sketchy and outdated. For instance, the 1970 census reported that 75.5 percent of Korean-American males and 41.5 percent of females over 16 years old were gainfully employed. Studies of the Korean immigrants by Kim and Condon in 1974 and by Kim, Sawdey, and Meihoefer in 1978–1979 in Chicago and Los Angeles showed a much higher percentage of labor force participation for both men (90 percent) and women (69 percent).[11] Unfortunately, accurate and reliable statistics on the employment, occupational status, and income levels of the Korean-American population are not currently available, and we must wait for the tabulation of the 1980 census. In the absence of any meaningful and reliable data, general observation of these variables will be offered.

In spite of their high educational achievement, a majority of the Korean immigrants are employed at middle-level positions such as proprietors and skilled and semi-skilled jobs.[12] In the Korean-American community, there is a consensus that many immigrants suffer from underemployment. It is not uncommon to find Korean Americans with college degrees working as filling station attendants or seamstresses in garment factories. The 1974 and 1978–1979 studies by Kim and others explored this subject by asking the subjective views of the respondents and by comparing their educational and occupational levels in Korea with their present occupations. Downward mobility of those who held jobs prior to immigration could be clearly established.[13]

Occupation and income levels are often closely related. They affect life choices and ultimately affect how people feel about themselves. Income data reported in the 1970 census are outdated because the majority of the Korean Americans in the United States in 1981 were not even living in the United States in 1970.

Data from the studies of Kim and others suggest that few Korean-American families are living below the poverty level, but that in most families, both parents are working full-time outside the home. The combined family income figures may thus conceal the substandard earnings of 2 wage earners.

The important consideration affecting the educational needs of Korean-American children is that, in most cases, both parents are absent from the home for some part of the day. Child care arrangements are problematic. Often informal child care arrangements are made with neighbors, or parents work in shifts to take care of their children. The responsibilities for the care and supervision of children fall to the parent who works the night shift.

Language Use and English Proficiency Level

Language use and English proficiency are extremely important variables that affect all aspects of the adjustment and occupational and economic success of Korean immigrants in the United States. According to the July 1975 Language Survey, 95 percent of the Korean-American respondents claim Korean to be their mother tongue.[14] Further, 55 percent of them used it as their major medium of communication. Kim and others' 1978–1979 study in Los Angeles and Chicago indicates even more extensive usage of Korean among the family members: over 75 percent of all spousal communication was exclusively in Korean and only a slightly smaller proportion of the parent-child communication was in Korean. Even within those families where English was used, the major portion of all communication was in Korean. As they lengthen their stay in the United States, however, selective use of English between parents and children occurs more frequently; but spousal communication remains almost exclusively in Korean. There is a positive relationship between the educational level of the parents and the use of English at home, i.e., the higher the educational level of the parents, the more English was used at home in combination with Korean.[15]

In this connection, it is important to note a strong tendency for Korean Americans to prefer extensive, or even exclusive, use of the Korean language when speaking to other Koreans. One major reason that the Korean language is preferred is that it is well-equipped to express vertical hierarchical social relationships. It is important to most Koreans to maintain these role relationships, particularly within the structure of the family. Since Korean Americans tend to retain extensive use of Korean, the English fluency of this group may increase at a relatively slow rate among the adult population, unless outside sources of English instruction and other incentives are provided.

Religious Preferences

Korean immigrants are predominantly Christian, with 60 percent Protestant and from 10 percent to 15 percent Catholic; less than 10 percent are Buddhist. It has been noted by many community leaders and in many studies that the roles of religious institutions in Korean-American communities go beyond the spiritual and religious ones.[16] These institutions provide social and emotional support and informal help, and they directly and indirectly serve as acculturation agents at the same time that they help preserve traditional values and heritage.

Summary: Profile of Korean Americans as a Group

To summarize, the demographic profile of Korean Americans indicates that they are not a particularly large group, although their numbers are increasing steadily as a result of immigration. In general, Korean Americans are well-educated, tend to be underemployed, have arrived in the United States in the last 10 years, and culturally are still predominantly Korean—particularly with regard to language preference.

As a group, Korean Americans display qualities of hard work, rugged individualism, adaptability, self-confidence, and strong faith in the American dream of unlimited opportunity for all. This is not to say that Korean Americans are without problems: they have problems and they are very real, but those problems and their consequences have to do with mental health, pursuit of happiness, and achievement of full human potential, rather than with absolute socioeconomic survival. Observers who have spent much time in Korean-American communities have little trouble identifying problem areas in these categories.

1. *Underemployment, with consequent frustration and loss of sense of worth.* This frustration and loss may lead to parenting problems, since the parent feels inadequate in the role of breadwinner and model for the children.

2. *Parent-child conflicts based on language and culture.* The children frequently expand their knowledge and use of English faster than the parents. As a result, the children become impatient with the parents, and the parents feel they have lost control in the family relationship.

3. *Breakdown of the traditional 3-generation Korean family.* No longer can the clearly defined roles and expectations in the traditional family be counted on as a source of strength in difficult and stressful times: the elderly feel lost and useless, parents no longer feel in a position of authority and sense that they are ineffective as role models, and children feel the loss of firm family expectations, but have no alternative system of guidance to replace them.

4. *A "lost generation" of teenage immigrants.* These are individuals who have failed to achieve positive self-identity from either Korean or American culture.

5. *A desire for biculturality, but no real sense of how to achieve it or what problems it entails.* In an age of cultural pluralism, biculturalism is a new area for both the minority and majority cultures to explore.

6. *Conflicting and unrealistic expectations for one's children.* The desire to preserve aspects of Korean culture often puts pressure on Korean-American children to behave in ways that are dysfunctional, especially if children are to satisfy other parental pressures toward academic success and economic mainstreaming.

7. *Major role shifts within the Korean family.* In an economic situation where both parents must work, and where there is increasing pressure from the children to communicate in English, family roles may shift rapidly and in ways that puzzle and frustrate the participants.

8. *Domestic violence such as child abuse and wife beatings.* These difficulties are symptomatic both of the frustration facing Korean-American immigrants and of loss of direction arising from the breakdown of
the traditional family structure and a shift in role expectations.

Compounded by all the usual stresses suffered by a visible minority
immigrant group attempting to adapt to life in a new and radically different
cultural setting, these problems also affect the educational adjustment and
achievement of the Korean-American child in the American public school.

EDUCATIONAL NEEDS AND PROBLEMS OF
KOREAN-AMERICAN CHILDREN AND YOUTH

It is extremely difficult to estimate the exact numbers of the percentage
of school-age children of Korean ancestry in American schools, although
current estimates are set at about 80,000.[17] Whatever the exact numbers,
the Korean-American children in public schools are comprised of both
American-born and foreign-born students, the majority of which are
foreign-born. Our discussion of the educational needs and problems of the
Korean-American students recognizes the different educational needs of
these 2 types of Korean-American children.

American-Born Korean-American Children and Youth

Educational issues for American-born children center around their
need to develop a positive bicultural identity amid the contrary forces of the
parents and American schools. It is safe to assume that these children have
been exposed to both English and Korean at home, but that Korean
predominates. Therefore, special instruction in English may be needed.
Their home environment, no matter how well-acculturated the parents may
be, will be primarily Korean. The family meals, cultural values, and
behavioral expectations and norms governing family interactions are more
likely to be Korean, as will be the medium of communication.

Korean-American parents strongly desire and expect their children to
show certain traditional Korean values and behavior traits at school: obedience, respectful deference to adults, and a generally passive stance toward
the learning experience. In practice, this may mean that the child does not
receive sufficient attention in the American classroom, where children are
expected to ask questions, speak out, and generally initiate much more
communication with the teacher. This may lead to further problems between parent and child, since the parent has very high expectations for the

child's academic achievement. More conflicts may arise later, because the parents have a narrow range of career expectations for their children, almost all of them highly professional: physician, lawyer, and engineer. A child who becomes acculturated to the American ideal of self-determination in career choices may be in for a head-on conflict.

At present, there are no role models or well-tested paths to develop a healthy bicultural identity for Korean-American school age children and youth. The Korean-American community will have to develop a system of choices and compromises between the 2 cultures. In turn, this system of choice and compromise may have direct consequences for the well-being of the individual (mainly with respect to the sense of marginality it engenders).[18] It may also have an important impact on the relationship of parent and child, both in terms of intergenerational conflict and reduced parenting effectiveness, because of the parents' own difficulties in clarifying cultural choices and compromises.

It may not be sufficient, however, to consider the intergenerational conflicts and parenting problems of Korean Americans solely in terms of parent-child relationship. The pertinent relationship may very well be the triadic one formed by the parent, the child, and the child's public school environment.[19]

Korean-Born (or Foreign-Born) Children and Youth

The overriding educational need of foreign-born children and youth is an effective bilingual program which promotes rapid acquisition of English while simultaneously maintaining the home language. Such a program facilitates the learning of grade-appropriate subject materials through both English and the home language. In this connection, the age of the foreign-born Korean student is an important consideration because it affects his or her educational needs and suggests an appropriate educational approach. For instance, the ease of second-language acquisition and the amount of subject materials to be mastered vary according to grade level. It has been observed that the younger the child, the easier it is for him/her to adapt and achieve grade-level learning.

The problems of foreign-born Korean students of junior and senior high school age are serious. Problems arise from many sources: some of them are age-related and others are associated with the immigration process, but the most powerful source of stress is the American public school, its milieu (peer groups and school personnel), and its curriculum. Let us examine these problems more closely.

First, puberty and adolescence is a difficult age in any culture and society. This is the period when exploration of identity and psychological independence from parents begins. Peer relationships and peer support are critical to achieving positive self-identity. Korean youth who immigrate to the United States leave behind these important relationships, which could provide them with a patterned way of dealing with many adolescent conflicts and problems. They come into a totally new culture and society without adequate English preparation to achieve a culturally congruent personal identity. In the American public schools, they are exposed to overt expressions of aggression and sexuality that, for the most part, were held in abeyance in their home country. Peer relationships, particularly heterosexual relationships, pose serious emotional and social challenges for these youth. They simply do not know how to behave or handle themselves in such relationships.

Their behavior toward adults or persons in authority positions also poses problems, particularly in a school setting. Their quiet, respectful behavior in the classroom is often regarded as showing a lack of initiative, or, even worse, it is interpreted as a sign of ignorance or failure to comprehend the subject matter. If the Korean-American youth adapt to the school's expectations, then their newly learned behavior of assertiveness from school gets them into severe conflicts with their parents who still expect obedience and respect from their children. Parents who are undergoing culture shock themselves feel offended and hurt by the "Americanized" behavior of their offspring. The fact that most of these young people survive such problems without serious emotional breakdowns is a miracle.

Because Korean parents and children alike value academic learning and high achievement, any academic difficulty or failure, regardless of its origin, causes extreme discouragement and depression. The suffering of Korean-American youth in their first year in American public school is often heartbreaking. Both academic help and educational counseling are needed for these youths and their parents to help them develop realistic educational expectations and goals for the first few years in America. Further support and reassurance must be provided: children will achieve desired academic success within a reasonable time, but not in the first month or year. Perhaps in this connection it is important to mention that Kim and others found in their 1978–1979 study that a majority of the Korean parents were satisfied with the American schools, but they wanted them to be more academically rigorous.

According to several bilingual teachers in the Los Angeles and Chicago schools, the most pressing needs of this age group are for grade-appropriate, Korean-language teaching materials. Existing English as a second language (ESL) materials are geared for lower-grade students and therefore are unsuitable for teenagers even though their English language levels may be low. Careful study and comparison of the curricula and teaching methods used in the Korean and American educational systems should be made when developing teaching materials for this age group. While some subject areas such as mathematics can be taught with English textbooks and some translation, and music and art can be taught with Korean textbooks, other subjects such as social studies and American history require extensive translation of the English textbooks into Korean. Many bilingual teachers spend their personal time and money to develop teaching materials to compensate for this lack.

In order to deal with the lowered self-esteem, anxiety, depression, and anger of Korean-American youth, individual and group counseling and educational guidance are sorely needed, particularly for children in the upper grades. And, obviously, the best persons should be bilingual and bicultural Korean-American professionals who would be familiar with the problems.

PARENTS' ATTITUDE TOWARD AND INVOLVEMENT WITH CHILDREN'S EDUCATION

Kim and others study in 1978–1979 clearly indicated that the parents studied were both concerned about and involved with their children's school experience.[20] They had high expectations and standards for their children, and they supported them by taking an active interest in their children's progress, by keeping close track of their children's performance, and, often, by tutoring their children at home to aid them in their school-work.

The study showed that the overall communication between parent and child appeared to be working well. For the most part, the parents were clearly communicating their expectations of and their satisfaction (or dissatisfaction) with their children, and, in turn, the children were clearly communicating their perception of the school experience to their parents. Thus there appeared to be no serious estrangement between parent and child, and, in turn, both parents and children had generally positive feelings about the public school.

However, there were some areas of difficulty. The parents had a sense that they were underemployed and/or underpaid and, more generally, that they were encountering some difficulties in gaining success and acceptance in America because of their Korean ethnicity. This tended to intensify the parents' feeling that it was very important for their children to learn English and adapt to the American majority culture so that their children would be assured of the success and acceptance that had been difficult for the parents themselves to attain.

Parental pressure of this sort may have serious consequences because the parents also strongly wanted their children to retain many Korean cultural traits, including extensive use of the Korean language for intra-ethnic communication. In many cases, the parents were not consciously aware of the incipient conflict, thus exacerbating it when it did occur.

It is apparent that, in most cases, the achievement of biculturality has to be managed through conscious choice; it will not come about on its own. For example, some parents experience anxiety when they stress Korean culture or the use of Korean language in the home, because they have a sense that this may impair their children's acquisition of English, which is also very important to the parents. It will take conscious effort and some guidance from persons who have already undergone bicultural adaptation in order for parents to come to terms with the choices they must make and the integration they must accomplish between the 2 cultures.

NEEDS OF TEACHERS OF KOREAN-AMERICAN CHILDREN

The 1978–1979 study by Kim and others also found that different teachers had greatly varying levels of sensitivity to the problems of the foreign-born, Korean-American child.[21] In general, however, the teachers had positive feelings toward Korean-American children: they were seen as causing no trouble, as pliable, and as highly motivated to learn. Also, the teachers took a good deal of pride in the progress made by most Korean-American children in mastering English. Finally, the teachers perceived nearly all the Korean-American parents as positive, concerned, and in-volved in their children's school experience.

On the negative side of the balance, many teachers felt they lacked sufficient information about the children's cultural background. One poten-tially severe problem area was uncovered in the study of the teachers: the teachers' highly favorable opinions of Korean-American children were due, in part, to comparing them with other minority children. At most of the schools in the study, many of the students who were not Korean were members of other minority groups, primarily Black and Hispanic. The study questionnaire was not designed to explore these comparative judg-ments, but it was clear from the teachers' responses that they often viewed the Korean-American children in a favorable light because they did not exhibit the learning and behavioral problems which they believed were common to the other minority children in the schools.

There are 2 potential dangers in this attitude. First, the Korean-American children may begin to sense that they are being praised at the expense of other minority children. The result may be that the Korean-American children may come to look down on other minorities. Second, the Korean-American children may acquire a false sense of their own capabilities and of the ease with which they are accepted by the majority culture. They may be in for a severe shock when they later attempt to compete on equal terms with the majority society, either at college or in the business and professional world.

Overall, the study found the intentions of the teachers to be positive and their efforts sincere. However, they often had difficulty in translating goodwill into effective action in the form of classroom programs that could be of real assistance to Korean-American children. Rarely had teachers developed any specific programs for the Korean-American children in their classes; still more rarely had any use been made of parents or other ethnic community resources in the classroom.

POSSIBLE FUTURE DEVELOPMENTS

Now that this paper has outlined the demographic characteristics and educational needs and problems of Korean-American children and youth, a philosophical question can be asked: what will be the future development for the Korean-American community and its people, particularly its children and youth?

As has been noted, there is no way to predict exactly what sort of cultural adaptation will finally be achieved by the new Korean immigrants in America, but one can outline the possibilities open to them. Being a visible minority, one option that is *not* open to Korean Americans is that of "passing for White," of totally submerging their ethnic distinctness, and becoming unnoticeable in American society. Another alternative that is open to them would be withdrawal into an ethnic enclave where they could preserve a hermetic version of their ethnic culture. This seems unlikely even at this early date: Korean Americans appear generally to opt for economic mainstreaming and, often, the upward-mobile move to the suburbs. Eliminating these possibilities leaves Korean Americans with 2 likely alternatives: marginality and biculturality. In short, will most Korean Americans fall between 2 cultures, ending up with no compelling ties to either, or will they succeed in developing a strong and viable biculturality, drawing upon and integrating the most positive aspects of both Korean and American culture?

Kim and others' 1978–1979 study found a strong foundation upon which Korean Americans could develop a dynamic biculturality.[22] There was much implicit cultural ambivalence on the part of the parents, but there was also a strong awareness of the importance of cultural influences on their parenting role and an intense desire to help their children to a successful future in America. The children proved to be bright, hard working, and usually successful in their mastery of the new environment. Finally, the public schools were found to be receptive to innovative thinking in the area of cultural adaptation. Overall, there were many positive resources apparent for the development of Korean-American biculturality, and there were no insurmountable negative forces present.

This is not to say, however, that a healthy biculturality will develop automatically, on its own, from these resources. The studies of Kim and others also showed many potential areas of conflict.[23] Rarely do those affected understand the positive steps that they must take to bring about a healthy resolution of differences: parents often are unaware that they must make conscious cultural choices; children sometimes cannot grasp the viable cultural alternatives offered to them by their parents; and public school personnel often do not realize the powerful part played by the children's school experience in influencing—or forcing—cultural choices. The cultural future of Korean Americans has much to build on, many positive forces that can be harnessed to achieve true biculturality. We must note, however, that there is much urgency in the situation: if Korean Americans are not helped to take advantage of their resources for biculturality, then this may be an opportunity forever lost. A generation from now it may be difficult, if not impossible, for this group to backtrack and attempt to retrieve a cultural heritage that can today be incorporated as a living component of a healthy biculturality.

REFERENCES

1. This is a conservative estimate, derived by applying the proportion of school-age children in the Korean-American population reported in the 1970 census to the probable present Korean-American population. That this figure is fairly accurate is indicated by the results of the 1976 Survey of Income and Education, which estimated that there were at that time 31,000 children of Korean-language background, aged 6–18. See National Center for Educational Statistics, *Bulletin* 78B-5, August 22, 1978, Table 1b.

2. According to the U.S. Census, there were 354,529 Korean ancestry immigrants and Americans in the United States at the time of the 1980 census taking. Undercounting of the Korean Americans is a serious problem shared by all minority racial groups—the percentage of undercounting of each racial minority group is not yet determined, but it is expected to be over 8 percent. Even if we were to disregard the undercount and growth rate through birth, an annual addition of over 30,000 new immigrants from Korea make the total population of the

Korean Americans to be 420,000 in 1982. A commonly accepted figure among the Korean American community is one-half million.

3. As of May 1982, the U.S. Census Bureau has not yet published demographic characteristics of immigrants and Americans of Korean ancestry (based on the 1980 census) except for their total number and their geographic distribution. Therefore, for the purpose of describing demographic characteristics of the Korean-American community, the author relied on the 1970 census figures and the data from the Annual Report of the Immigration and Naturalization Services. Unfortunately, the Service ceased its publications in 1978.

4. Bok-Lim C. Kim, *The Asian Americans: Changing Patterns, Changing Needs,* (Montclair, NJ: Association of Korean Christian Scholars, 1978); Bok-Lim C. Kim, Michael Sawdey, and Barbara Meihoefer, *The Korean American Child at School and at Home, an Analysis of Interaction and Intervention through Groups* (Project Report, September 30, 1978-June 30, 1980, Urbana, IL: University of Illinois, School of Social Work).

5. Public Law 80-236, October 1965, abolished the long standing inequitable quota system which discriminated against immigrants from Asia.

6. Bernice B.H. Kim, "The Koreans in Hawaii," *Social Science* 9 (4) (October 1934): 410.

7. The practice of exchanging pictures of a prospective bride and groom as a preliminary step in arranged marriages was common among the Korean and Japanese societies during the late nineteenth and early twentieth centuries. This practice was heavily relied on in the early 1920s by the young Korean and Japanese immigrant men in the United States and by their parents in the home country. Cross-Pacific ocean travel for the purpose of courtship and marriage was both costly and legally problematic because of the restrictive U.S. immigration policy toward immigrants from Asia. The term "picture bride" thus came about because of the extensive use of pictures for the matrimonial decision. With this system, the groom's picture was used during the marriage ceremony in the home country before the bride embarked on her long journey to join her husband whom she had never met. For further information on this subject, read Chin Kim and Bok-Lim C. Kim, "Asian Immigrants in American Law: A Look at the Past and the Challenge which Remains," *American University Law Review* 26 (2) (Winter 1977): 373–407.

8. For documentation of legal discrimination, read Kim and Kim, cited above in note 7.

9. For instance, in 1959, the year when the Immigration and Naturalization Service began to desegregate Korean immigrants by age and sex, one-third of the total immigrants (1,717) were children under 4 years of age and an additional 12.6 percent were under 9 years of age. A figure of 26.5 percent of the female immigrants between the ages of 20–29 clearly represent intermarried Korean women. For further information see Bok-Lim C. Kim, "An Emerging Immigrant Community, Korean Americans," *Civil Rights Digest* (1976): 40.

10. Ki-Taek Chun, "The Myth of Asian American Success and Its Educational Ramifications," *IRCD Bulletin* 15 (1 & 2) (Winter/Spring 1980); Bok-Lim C. Kim and M. Condon, *A Study of Asian Americans in Chicago: Their Socioeconomic Characteristics, Problems and Service Needs, Final Report to NIMH;* Kim, Sawdey, Meihoefer, *The Korean American Child at School, and at Home.*

11. Kim, Sawdey, and Meihoefer, p. 28, Tables II-10 and II-11; p. 57, Tables III-7 and III-8.

12. Kim, Sawdey, and Meihoefer, pp. 58–59.

13. Kim, *The Asian Americans: Changing Patterns, Changing Needs.* pp. 185–86.

14. U.S. Department of Commerce, Bureau of the Census, *Current Population Reports Special Studies,* Series P-23 No. 60 (Revised) (Washington, DC: U.S. Government Printing Office, July 1976), p. 3.

15. Kim, Sawdey, and Meihoefer, pp. 29 and 60.

16. Hyung-Chan Kim, ''The History and Role of the Church in the Korean American Community,'' in *The Korean Diaspora* (Santa Barbara, CA: Clio Press, 1977), pp. 47–63.

17. See note 1.

18. D.W. Sue, ''Ethnic Identity: The Impact of Two Cultures on the Psychological Development of Asians in America,'' In *Asian Americans Psychological Perspectives,* ed. by S. Sue and N. Wagner, (Palo Alto: CA, Science and Behavior, 1973).

19. L.C. Hirata, ''Youth, Parents and Teachers in Chinatown: A Triadic Framework of Minority Socialization,'' *Urban Education,* 10 (1975): 279, 296.

20. Bok-Lim C. Kim, Michael Sawdey, and Barbara Meihoefer, *The Korean-American Child at School and at Home: An Analysis of Interaction and Intervention through Groups* (Project Report, September 30, 1978–June 30, 1980: Urbana, IL, University of Illinois, School of Social Work).

21. Kim, Sawdey, and Meihoefer, p. 84.

22. Kim, Sawdey, and Meihoefer, p. 78.

23. Kim, Sawdey, and Meihoefer.

Socioeconomic Issues Affecting the Education of Minority Groups: The Case of Filipino Americans

by Federico M. Macaranas

Filipino Americans comprise the second largest American group of Asian origin today. The growth of this community was initially linked to the unskilled labor needs of Hawaii and the West Coast during the early twentieth century, but with the marked changes in the American economy and society through 2 world wars and one major depression, immigration policy altered the size and composition of the local Filipino population.

The surge in the entry of professionals from the Philippines, which occurred after the 1965 liberalization of immigration laws, inevitably led to today's heterogeneous Filipino-American community, one that is quite diverse in many aspects, including the educational. Thus, this ethnic group appears like a detail from the larger American mosaic—as colorful and complex as the whole—suggesting that education practitioners may have to adopt several perspectives when they are involved with students, faculty, or staff from this burgeoning community.

This paper attempts to summarize the most salient socioeconomic issues pertaining to the education of Filipino Americans, given the diversity within the community itself. The first section briefly reviews the growth of this ethnic group through the 1970s and the experience of the so-called first wave of immigrants. The social demography of the second wave is then examined, focusing on characteristics of professionals who have increasingly accounted for the post-1965 influx. Major education-related issues are thereafter discussed; highlighted are the debates on the cultural-deficit theory which purportedly explains Filipino-American attitudes towards education; the social indicators of equity in education for 1960, 1970, and 1976; and the differences in native- versus foreign-born students. Finally,

the future educational needs of the community are presented, and suggestions for a deeper understanding of Filipino-American students are made.

HISTORICAL OVERVIEW

Filipinos first came to the Americas by way of the colonial route, not
through the U.S., surprisingly enough, but through the Spanish imperial
domain. Spain ceded the Philippines to the U.S. in 1898 by the Treaty of
Paris (which also ended the Spanish-American War). Before this time,
there had been an active trade between the Philippines and Mexico. Thus,
the earliest Filipinos in the U.S. were sailors of the Manila-Acapulco
galleon trade who jumped ship because of the brutish treatment they had
received from the Spaniards, crossed the Gulf of Mexico, and settled in
Louisiana in the mid-eighteenth century.[1] By the turn of the twentieth
century, there were some 2,000 Filipinos in the New Orleans area, but they
were not separately identified in the Bureau of Census counts because of
definitional restrictions on immigrant populations.

The colonial status of the Philippines explains the origin of 2 types of
immigrants who to this day, by the very nature of their employment, are
visible as expatriate communities. In 1907, approximately 150 Filipinos
were recruited to work in Hawaiian sugar planatations. Their numbers
easily rose to the thousands when other sources of cheap labor were no
longer accessible due to the 1882 Chinese Exclusion Act; the 1907 U.S.
immigration law barring recruitment from Portugal, Spain, and Puerto
Rico; and the 1908 Gentlemen's Agreement with Japan.[2] There were
approximately 19,000 Filipinos recruited by the Hawaii Sugar Planters
Association (HSPA) by 1915, another 14,000 in the next 5 years, and some
39,000 in the 2 succeeding 5-year periods. Altogether the HSPA recruited
approximately 126,000 Filipinos between 1907 and 1946.[3]

Even before the time that cheap, unskilled farm labor was being
recruited by the HSPA, Filipino seamen started to appear as stewards in the
U.S. Navy, not only to escape rural poverty but also to enter adventurous
lives abroad. In 1903, 9 of them were listed in this rank. By 1905, the
number had risen to 178; by 1917 it had reached 2,000; and after World War
I, it had stabilized at around 4,000.[4] A third group of potential immigrants,
young scholars sent to the U.S. for further studies (some 103
"pensionados" [pensioned students] in 1903 alone), did not materialize
since they returned home after completing their programs.

Census data show that the Filipino population in the U.S. grew from
21,000 in 1920 to 108,000 in 1930. Through 1934, most migrants were

dominantly young, single, unskilled males typically employed either as farm laborers in Hawaii, California, or Washington; or as domestics or personal service workers (bellboys, busboys, dishwashers); or as salmon cannery laborers in Alaska. The recruitment practices led to an imbalance in sex ratios (which, for example, averaged 12 men per Filipino women between 1909 and 1934), as men with rural backgrounds and low education were preferred over others.[5] This explains why 1970 census statistics showed the median years of schooling completed by Filipino males 65 years and over was only 5.4 years, and why many of them never married. The recruitment strategy also explains the pivotal role of taxi dance halls in the lives of many male immigrants and possibly in anti-Filipino race riots.[6]

In 1940, the Filipino population dipped to 98,000. Smith reported that the median years of schooling for mainland Filipinos were 7.4, while only 7.7 percent of those 25 years old and over had some college education, attributable to the fact that the immigrants came from the same pool as in the earlier decades.[7] In contrast, Allen found the corresponding data for 1970 to be 13.5 median years of schooling and that 43.2 percent of those 25 years old and over had some college education.[8]

These dramatic changes were brought about by the immigration policy of nationality quotas (in effect between 1934 and 1965) and a liberalized 1965 act which enabled Filipinos with particular skills to enter the U.S. on a basis other than family reunion. While national origin quotas were set in 1924, it wasn't until 1934, with the passage of the Philippine Independence Act, that Filipino migration to the U.S. was curtailed to 50 persons per year. The 1924 quota policy had imposed limits on Latin and Slavic immigrants and barred the inflow of anyone of Asiatic origin except Filipinos (who had been classified as U.S. nationals, since the Philippines were a U.S. colony). Not unexpectedly, exclusion sentiments against Filipinos ran high, and their noncitizen status precluded them from enjoying more than the most fundamental rights. Described as "neither fish nor fowl," Filipinos were victimized by vigilante groups fearful of the economic and social competition fostered by the presence of non-Whites injecting "mongrel" strains into the country.[9] On top of this were various forms of institutional discrimination, such as antimiscegenation laws, exclusion from federal relief projects during the depression, police harassment, and segregation practices in public places as well as in real estate and housing.

Not until after World War II was the annual Philippine quota of 50 immigrants raised to 100. Filipinos who fought with Americans during this war qualified as nonquota immigrants under the amendment of the Nationality Act, dated March 27, 1942, which provided for the expeditious nationalization of all aliens in the service of the U.S. Armed Forces. However, the Commissioner of Immigration and Naturalization, in a letter to the Attorney General dated September 13, 1945, deliberately excluded Filipinos from this provision despite their gallant service under the American flag during World War II. The Filipinos were the only nationality to be so discriminated against. This policy reversal has yet to be rectified.

The accelerated growth of the Filipino community in the U.S. after World War II can best be visualized from Figure 1, taken from Allen.[10] American-born Filipino Americans (36 percent of whom resided in the mainland in 1950, versus 0.9 percent in 1940) helped raise the population figures to 123,000 by 1950, to 182,000 by 1960, and to 336,000 by 1970. The 1976 Survey of Income and Education reported 554,000 Filipinos in the U.S., 34 percent of whom were American-born. Data from the 1980 census reveal some 775,000 Filipinos in the U.S.,[11] a quarter of a million shy of the projections by Owan in 1975[12] and consistent with the prediction that this community would outnumber the Japanese community in the U.S. by 1980. (See Figure 1 at the end of this chapter.)

The demand for educational resources will therefore increase significantly in the 1980s, particularly for language education. (See Table 1.) Language concerns will be especially prominent in certain standard metropolitan statistical areas as families reunite and cluster in Filipino neighborhoods. Although most post-1965 immigrants have begun to settle in other parts of the country, in 1974 the West still accounted for over 70 percent of Filipinos in the U.S., where they mainly reside in California, Hawaii, and Washington.[13] Illinois, New York, Virginia, New Jersey, Ohio, Pennsylvania, and Maryland are the other major areas of Filipino concentration, chiefly in urban centers. (See Table 2.)

The invisibility of the Filipino community due to "weakly nucleated settlement patterns [contrasting] with the racial segregation of the pre-World War II period in West Coast cities"[14] is fast turning into fiction; a cursory investigation of regional and town associations reported in Filipino-American newspapers shows this, especially in California urban areas. It can be safely conjectured that, compared to 1970, there will be more tracts in the 1980 census with over 10 percent Filipinos.

SOCIAL DEMOGRAPHY

The Immigration Act of 1965 which became fully effective in 1968 created several categories of preference systems under which new migrants could come into the U.S. Annual reports of the Immigration and Naturalization Service Commissioner reveal 2 general classes of Filipino immi-grants. The first group, who comprise over 40 percent of the Filipino immigrants who enter each year, fall into the first, second, fourth, and fifth preference categories, which concern the reuniting of families. The remain-der of these immigrants come into the country mostly under the third and sixth preference categories, which are granted for occupational reasons. Concerning the latter types of immigrants, and professionals in the former categories as well, many researchers have come up with a variety of explanations about the factors behind the decision to migrate, including environmental factors such as the political/economic environment and human resource needs of the Philippines and the U.S.; demographic factors such as occupation, sex, college course taken, college attended, employer, source of support for U.S. study, citizenship of spouse; and socio-psycho-logical factors such as career salience, need for achievement, personal values, and ties to the Philippines or the U.S.[15] A National Science Founda-tion survey in 1974 on immigrant engineers and scientists from the Philip-pines indicates that this brain drain is largely attributable to "pull" factors such as better opportunities for children and higher standards of living, and "push" factors such as low salaries, insufficient research opportunities, and poor advancement prospects in the Philippines. The political environ-ment was also among the most frequently rated "very important" factors explaining migration.

The post-1965 Filipino migration constitutes part of a "second wave" that is quite distinct from the agricultural migrants of low socioeconomic origin in the early decades of this century. Most of those immigrants could really be thought of as sojourners who "had hoped naively to accumulate large earnings, acquire an education, and then return home."[16] Profession-als constituted less than 2 percent of all Filipinos in the U.S. in 1940 and 1950, but immigration in the 1960s changed this picture dramatically: 48 percent of immigrants in 1961–65 were professionals, a figure that rose to 60 percent in 1966–68 and 69 percent in 1969–72.[17] Similar data for 1973–75 show a drop in the professionals' percentage share to 58 percent but an increase in white-collar immigrants to 17 percent, up from the 10 percent registered in 1969–72.[18]

The impact that the newer wave of migrants had on the 1970 national percentage for Filipino men who had completed college (15 percent) can be seen when these figures are compared with the U.S. average for men (13 percent) and when it is considered that there were a number of older uneducated Filipinos in the population. Between 1960 and 1970, Filipino male professionals tripled. In the 1970s, the Philippines were the most important source of new immigrant professionals.

Filipino women continue to have the highest completion rates for high school and college among women in any population group. In 1970, 55 percent of them were in the labor force, compared to 36 percent a decade earlier; one third of them were classified as professionals in 1970. This proportion could increase through the 1980s because of the large influx of professionals in general.

The new wave of migration has led to more Filipino families with younger children. Between 1968–1976, when Filipinos increased their share of total immigration to the U.S. from below 4 percent to above 9 percent, typically one out of 3 or 4 immigrants every year was aged 19 years or below, and between 11–20 percent were 9 years old or less.[19] The geographical distribution of the first and second waves naturally extend themselves to the scatter of school-age Filipinos across the country, but socioeconomic factors conspire against interregional uniformity in the percentage enrollment for various age groups. In 1970, for example, the South had lower than the national average for Filipino-American school enrollment in all age groups, except for females in the 14–17 age bracket. Compared to all Filipinos in the U.S., the South also had a lower median or mean income for families and also lower income per person and a greater percentage of all persons with income at less than poverty level.

EDUCATION ISSUES

The Cultural Deficit Theory

Two age groups present disturbing underenrollment for school statistics. In 1970, the 14.5 percent preschool enrollment rate of Filipinos between 3–4 years old, though above the U.S. average, was much lower than that of the Chinese and Japanese communities (23.9 percent and 31.4 percent, respectively), despite the higher labor participation rate of Filipino women compared to any other group. These figures have been interpreted to be reflective of a need to open up more preschool opportunities,[20] thus presuming the existence of a demand for preparation for further schooling. Likewise, 1970 school enrollment figures for college-aged (18–24 years old) Filipino males (28 percent) and females (23 percent) were below the U.S. average rates (37 percent and 27 percent respectively) and even much lower than those of the Chinese (71 percent and 58 percent) and Japanese (56 percent and 48 percent). These figures are partly explained by an entry into the labor force[21] and earlier marriage.[22]

The school enrollment statistics bring to the fore the issue of the Filipino's alleged lack of experience with a traditional education system and the social organizations needed to support it.[23] "Unlike other minority groups which have *inherent* conducive controls for education, there has been little support or mechanism for educational advancement in both the individual Philippine-American home and the Philippine-American community as a whole," asserts Lott.[24] (Emphasis added.)

This cultural deficit argument runs counter to observations about the educational ambitions of the first wave Filipinos, which, for example, Bogardus (cited in Melendy)[25] found to be a major reason for positive opinions by Caucasians of Filipinos during the California racial riots in the 1920s, and which the literary pen of Carlos Bulosan, a peasant immigrant, deftly and sympathetically portrayed in his works.[26] It also appears inconsistent with the post-World War II literacy rate and college enrollment ratios in the Philippines, which are among the highest in the world, and which inevitably lead to the generally high educational attainment of the second wave immigrants.[27]

The absence of "inherent conducive controls for education" in the Filipino community may not be attributed to the lack of experience with a traditional education system. Macaranas, citing historical studies of education between the sixteenth and early twentieth centuries, points out the fact that, prior to the colonization of the Philippines, a formal education tradition was very much alive in the country; there were schools where children were taught reading, writing, arithmetic (including the decimal system), religion and incantation, and fencing for self-defense.[28] Sanskrit was taught in the sourthern parts since it was the official language of Borneo with which trade was flourishing. It was the Spaniards who stunted higher learning for native Filipinos since most of the colleges and universities they established (the oldest antedates the founding of Harvard University) were reserved exclusively for the colonizers and their offspring. With the arrival of the Thomasites, American educators who came to democratize schooling in the Philippines in the early twentieth century, 3 centuries of Spanish neglect were corrected (although the curriculum contents were more American than Filipino, as critics rightly contend).

There are further pieces of evidence against the cultural deprivation thesis. Junasa, in a 1961 study of Filipino youth in Waipahu, Hawaii, concluded that a greater percentage of those planning to continue their schooling after graduation from high school were from families of higher socioeconomic background; this same conclusion was reached for the larger American society by Bowles and Gintis in 1976.[29] These studies suggest that deprivation is not cultural in origin but economic, unless one believes that poverty breeds a culture that is innately antieducation.[30]

Junasa also found that those youngsters who planned to further their studies had parents who expressed deep interest in the children's schooling by (1) keeping themselves informed of the progress of their children in school, (2) frequently encouraging their children to do better, and (3) expressing definite wishes to their children that they seek further schooling.[31] To the extent that the parents' socioeconomic statuses and their desires to have better educated children were predetermined by their own Philippine experiences, the educational system in the Philippines may be said to play an integral part in the economic problems of both waves of immigrants.

Poorly educated parents who have not broken the barriers to upward socioeconomic mobility in the U.S. may not prod their siblings to pursue higher education. Even the more educated parents may fail to motivate their children because of the problems they have faced as immigrant professionals, for example, discriminatory practices in the labor markets; licensing requirements; failure to get jobs due to alleged overqualifications in experience or in education (see Table 3, items 5 and 6), poor quality education, or working in areas which their educational backgrounds do not fit.[32]

These findings match those of Hune who argues that ''by continuing to view Philipinos as victims of cultural deprivation, historians and social scientists have overlooked their relationship with the larger American context.''[33] Another study that reinforces this viewpoint suggests that, because of noncultural factors, education does not affect income levels of Filipino Americans in any statistically significant way for the community as a whole.[34] The latter observation is once more in stark contrast to findings about other Asian-American groups, where the positive impact of schooling on the incomes of Chinese and Japanese communities is seen. (These differences are observed even after accounting for the separate impact on earnings of age, sex, and percentage of full-time workers in the ethnic group.) Such results can be explained in part by the differences in occupational achievements which intervene in the education-income line.[35] Fewer Filipinos are in the work category ''professional, technical, and kindred workers:'' why this is the case may be traced not only to the factors cited above but also to the length of the migration experience of the group.[36] This is definitely not cultural in character.

In support of the cultural deficit theory is the consumption view of education, i.e., schooling that is not an investment in human resources for maximizing personal earnings or returns at a future date. Economists have observed that the Philippine higher educational system is more highly oriented towards the less remunerative liberal arts than it is towards the sciences, which are needed for the economic development of the country. Profit-seeking private schools, which enroll 95 percent of college students, have been observed to offer courses

> . . . where capital investments and instructional costs per student are relatively low: commerce, business administration, teacher training, law and the liberal arts. Since these areas are the fields where enrollments can be multiplied without much additional investment, tuition and fees can be made relatively lower per student in these areas. In a country where the diploma is more important than the educational discipline, these would also be the most attractive areas for students who desire the status symbol and prestige of a college education since these can be purchased here at the lowest price.[37]

Cheetham and Hawkins also found for Philippine education that "quality is unsatisfactory in fields requiring relatively high costs per student (for example, engineering, a field in which many graduates fail in the professional examination)."[38]

The consumption view is not universally applicable to Filipinos in the U.S., however. A 1978 survey of predominantly second wave immigrants in the metropolitan New York area demonstrated that the respondents were conscious of the need for an investment-type of education in order to be able to succeed in the U.S.[39] The respondents, averaging 26 years old, were typically conscious of U.S. labor market discrimination and were entrepreneurial-minded.

The cultural deficit theory may also be supported by another survey of Filipinos in Stockton, California.[40] This 1980 study revealed that the predictors for full-time college attendance among females were single civil status, higher ethnic identification, less-educated father, intact family, positive maternal influence, greater age difference between father and mother and between mother and subject, greater flexibility, and higher measured intelligence. Similar predictors for males were single status, educated father, higher income expectations at age 30, less Filipino background of the paternal grandmother, smaller age difference between parents, and less socialization, which implied that ". . . they are less likely to conform to norms in society."[41] One need only disavow some of the predictors which may be justified as culturally rooted to explain the relatively low college attendance of Filipino males and females observed in the 1970 census; but there may be good grounds to believe that cultural traits have been shaped by economic circumstances.

Economic Assimilation and Education

In addition to the cultural deficit theory, another area of educational concern in the Filipino-American community is one involving the social indicators of equity in education. The data in Table 3 are rough measures of socioeconomic assimilation which Card, based on a 1980 study of Filipinos in the San Francisco Bay Area, found to be less rapid than cultural assimilation but more rapid than the structural type of assimilation (association with Caucasians). Indeed, in the 16-year period covered in the table, the figures indicate that the process of reaching parity with the male majority reference group has not been smooth (e.g., delayed education, high school completion and college overqualification indicators for males). In fact, there has been some retrogression in certain indicators for females (high school nonattendance and college overqualification indicators) which is related to the poor performance of Filipino women on the income side for the labor market.[42] Males appear to be improving in some indicators (lower percentages of delayed education and high school nonattendance, larger ratios for college completion and earnings differential for college-educated). However, these are weighed down by other indicators, not reported in Table 3, such as earnings mobility and mean earnings adjusted for age, educational attainment, prestige score for occupation, regional cost of living, and hours worked. There are other studies to support this dreary picture.

One study estimates that, while the initial income differential between Filipino immigrants and Hawaiian-born Filipino Americans is reduced by nearly one-half over their working lives, the "immigrants never overcome the disadvantages associated with foreign birth"—they never catch up in terms of income.[43] This is in direct contrast to the opposite result for European male immigrants, possibly because the Filipino immigrants have low median levels of education (4.5 years) relative to natives (11.5) and are mainly in menial occupations (40 percent versus 20 percent) that do not offer the upward mobility to raise their incomes.[44] Another study, in 1981, estimated that, among the native-born Filipino Americans, half of their lower earnings may be explained by differences in schooling (differences in experience and weeks worked played smaller roles).[45] More important was the finding that "the lower earnings and employment . . . arise from the smaller favorable impact of their human capital. At this point it is not clear whether these smaller favorable impacts arise from a lower quality of schooling and on-the-job training, or from a lower payoff from training of the same quality."[46]

Some problems of interpretation of the social indicators in Table 3 must be recognized. First, none of the indicators can purport to measure well-being, because no inputs or casual factors leading to the outcomes are assessed at all; instead, emphasis is placed on results, thus neglecting differences in access to resources available to various groups. Therefore, information on opportunities for resources must be considered, e.g., the impact of out-of-pocket costs on the high school and college completion rates and the local factors responsible for underemployment, so that educators may correct those resources under their control (e.g., curriculum matters, job placement assistance, counseling programs, etc.).[47]

Second, differences in native- versus foreign-born may mask problems or create them where none exist when data are lumped. For example, the brighter picture for Filipino Americans on the delayed education indicators may very well be due to the inclusion of recently arrived students continuing their education in the U.S. from the 6-year elementary, 4-year secondary cycles in the Philippines—2 years shy of the American standard. Age/grade placement problems have also been suggested as a possible cause for lack of interest in schooling.[48]

Pluralism and the Native- versus Foreign-Born

The language characteristics of foreign-born and American-born Filipinos in Table 1 show the following contrasting data: (1) While 95 percent of the foreign-born are from Pilipino-language backgrounds, this ratio stands at 65 percent for the native-born. (2) Of those with Pilipino-language backgrounds, 83 percent of the foreign-born are in Pilipino-language households compared to 88 percent for the other group. (3) Of those in Philpino-language households, English is the usual individual language in 58 percent of the foreign-born and 50 percent for the native-born.

These data manifest strong differences at the language background level but not at the household and individual language levels. The foreign-born Filipino American's proficiency in English, however, differs from individual to individual for several reasons. In the Philippines, students from non-Tagalog speaking regions (Tagalog being the basis of the national language, Pilipino) have the burden of learning English in addition to their native dialects and Pilipino. English is still used there as the medium of instruction in higher grades in primary schools as well as at secondary and collegiate levels all over the country. (There are over 70 dialects in the country.) The quality of instruction varies regionally, due to shortages in classrooms and textbooks. A continuous progression scheme was adopted in 1971 allowing every student to move into the next grade automatically until s/he completes the sixth year.[49] Hence, English as a second language (ESL) programs will be increasingly needed for these young students who, once enrolled in American schools, are confronted with a whole new world of problems, including unfamiliarity with testing methods.[50] See the Appendix at the end of this chapter for a list of concerns and needs relating to Filipino-American students, taken from Paula Y. Bagasao's study of a junior high school in Los Angeles.

Other differences between native- and foreign-born Filipinos in the U.S. range from outward manifestations in speech, clothing, and sociability to the ability to express and cope with aggression and the presence or absence of viable identification figures, such as parents and Filipino neighbors.[51] Differences such as these have been the sources of tension between the 2 groups, the "locals" and the "FOBs" (the "Fresh off the Boats," or the "Flip Overboards," or the "Fresh Off the Borders"). Those who have studied the situation, such as Amefil Agabayni, argue that one way to relieve such discord is for authorities to adopt cultural and language pluralism.[52]

The shift in most recent studies of the immigrant experience has been away from the assimilationist model towards the pluralist paradigm.[53] In the latter, ethnic groups are assumed to maintain group identification even to the third or fourth generations, whereas in the former they are thought to lose identity in the melting pot. Both models appear to be present in many Filipino homes, but the latter is more prominent in its implications for education issues, especially as they are viewed within older Filipino-American communities.[54] Through the Pilipino Far West Task Force on Education in California, the Filipino-American community has advised, formally and informally, on curriculum matters and school policies for children of kindergarten to college age.[55] Several master's theses and doctoral dissertations have been written on Filipino culture-specific issues and language problems.[56] Inadequate and inaccurate representations and references to Filipinos and the Philippines have been raised, and classroom materials dealing with Filipinos have been prepared for non-Filipino teachers.[57]

THE FUTURE

As second wave immigrants swell the ranks of Filipinos in the U.S., the diversity of the educational needs of the community will increase. For example, in response to the need of preschoolers, it is expected that more nurseries will be opened by enterprising Filipinos, particularly those with backgrounds in education and/or child psychiatry. Filipino academic achievers will gain more prominence in their own schools and high expectations may be imposed on their less gifted counterparts by teachers not sensitive to differences in their backgrounds—their nativity, prior Philippine schooling, parental support, etc.—which signals the need for programs to make educators more aware of such differences. In areas with high concentrations of Filipino Americans, bilingual/bicultural programs may be demanded more militantly by Filipino taxpayers.

The search for ethnic roots will more likely be initiated by third- and later-generation Filipino-Americans: they will demand more sensitivity to their historical interests through curricular reform, the formation of new associations which will engage in local and statewide politics, and research that will document the experiences of the various Filipino communities across the country.

Through the schools, churches, ethnic mass media, and regional associations, the socioeconomically assimilated members of the group will serve as role models for many of the newly arrived migrants and their children, but perhaps this will occur only within limited class lines.

The number of Filipinos in relatively low socioeconomic status may rise as the foreign-born experience the realities of their inadequate Philippine education and the sophisticated discriminatory practices in the labor markets, especially for professionals. Licensing requirements will be actively questioned by Filipino professional associations; they will provide more refresher and continuing education courses for their members. Finally, the need for a national lobbying group will gradually dawn on the community leaders as common issues are recognized.

FIGURE 1. Filipino Population Growth in the United States*

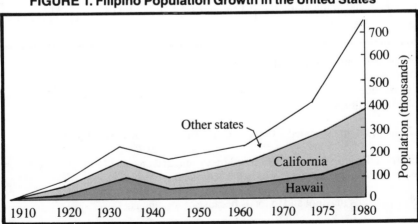

*Source: Adapted from James P. Allen, "Recent Immigration from the Philippines and Filipino Communities in the United States," *The Geographical Review* 11 (1) (1977): 195–208.

TABLE 1:   Estimated Number of Persons of Filipino Origin in the United States, by Place of Birth and Language Characteristics, Spring 1976*

(Numbers Are in Thousands)				
Language Characteristics	Total	Native-born	Foreign-born	
			Total	Philippines
Total	554 (1)	186	369 (2)	364
With English-language backgrounds	76	63	(*)	(*)
With Pilipino-language backgrounds	471	121	350	346
In English-only households	74	13	61	60
In Pilipino-language households	397 (3)	107	289	286
With English as usual individual language	222	54	168	166
With Pilipino as usual individual language	123	(*)	119	119

(*) Fewer than an estimated 15,000 persons.

(1) Includes an estimated 7,000 persons with non-English language backgrounds other than Pilipino.

(2) Includes an estimated 2,000 persons born abroad outside the Philippines.

(3) Includes an estimated 37,000 children younger than 4 and 15,000 other persons whose individual language was not ascertained.

Note: Details may not add to totals because of roundings.

---

*Source: Survey of Income and Education conducted by the Bureau of the Census, Spring 1976, as reported in the *National Center for Education Statistics Bulletin* 79-B-12, May 21, 1979.

TABLE 2: Geographical Distribution of Filipinos in the United States, 1980 and 1970*

	1980	1970	Change, 1970 to 1980 Number	Change, 1970 to 1980 Percent	Percent distribution 1980	Percent distribution 1970
United States. . .	774,640	343,060	431,580	125.8	100.0	100.0
Northeast	75,104	31,424	43,680	139.0	9.7	9.2
Massachusetts	3,073	2,361	712	30.2	0.4	0.7
Connecticut	3,132	2,177	955	43.9	0.4	0.6
New York.	33,956	14,279	19,677	137.8	4.4	4.2
New Jersey	24,377	5,623	18,754	333.5	3.1	1.6
Pennsylvania	8,267	4,560	3,707	81.3	1.1	1.3
North Central	79,945	27,824	52,121	187.3	10.3	8.1
Ohio	7,435	3,490	3,945	113.0	1.0	1.0
Indiana	3,625	1,365	2,260	165.6	0.5	0.4
Illinois	43,839	12,654	31,185	246.4	5.7	3.7
Michigan	11,162	3,657	7,505	205.2	1.4	1.1
Wisconsin	2,698	1,209	1,489	123.2	0.3	0.4
Minnesota	2,675	1,456	1,219	83,7	0.3	0.4
Missouri	4,029	2,010	2,019	100.4	0.5	0.6
Kansas	1,662	758	904	119.3	0.2	0.2
South	82,596	31,979	50,617	158.3	10.7	9.3
Maryland	10,965	5,170	5,795	112.1	1.4	1.5
Virginia	18,901	7,496	11,405	152.1	2.4	2.2
North Carolina	2,542	905	1,637	180.9	0.3	0.3
Georgia	2,792	1,253	1,539	122.8	0.4	0.4
Florida	14,212	5,092	9,120	179.1	1.8	1.5
Louisiana	2,614	1,249	1,365	109.3	0.3	0.4
Oklahoma	1,687	612	1,075	175.7	0.2	0.2
Texas	15,096	3,442	11,654	338.6	1.9	1.0
West	536,995	251,833	285,162	113.2	69.3	73.4
Colorado	2,901	1,068	1,833	171.6	0.4	0.3
Arizona	3,363	1,253	2,110	168.4	0.4	0.4
Utah	928	392	536	136.7	0.1	0.1
Washington	24,363	11,462	12,901	112.6	3.1	3.3
Oregon	4,257	1,633	2,624	160.7	0.5	0.5
California	357,514	138,859	218,655	157.5	46.2	40.5
Hawaii	133,964	93,915	40,049	42.6	17.3	27.4

*Source: U.S. Department of Commerce, Bureau of the Census, *1980 Census of Population Supplementary Reports Pc80-S1-3, Race of the Population by States: 1980,* July 1981.

TABLE 3: Social Indicators of Equity in Education for Asian-Americans, Raw Measures for 1960, 1970, and 1976, By Ethnic Group and Sex*

		Chinese	Japanese	Pilipino	Majority
1. Delayed education: percentage of 15-, 16- and 17-year olds who are two or more years behind the modal grade for their age on April 1	1960 M	13	5†	14	18
	F	6	8†	3†	10†
	1970 M	10	4†	13	12
	F	9	1†	7†	6†
	1976 M	na	8	7	10
	F	na	1†	3	7†
2. High school non-attendance: percentage of 15-, 16- and 17-year olds who were not enrolled in school on April 1	1960 M	9	2†	12	18
	F	14	3†	7	12†
	1970 M	6	6	8	9
	F	9	6	9	8
	1976 M	na	2	6	5
	F	na	1†	10	6
3. High school completion: percentage of persons from 20–24 years of age who have completed 12 or more years of school	1960 M	84†	89†	81†	69
	F	82†	84†	76	70
	1970 M	90†	94†	77†	83
	F	88†	94†	84	82
	1976 M	88	98†	81	87
	F	90	99†	78†	86

*Source: U.S. Commission on Civil Rights, *Social Indicators of Equality for Minorities and Women*, August 1978.

TABLE 3: Social Indicators of Equity (Continued)

4. College completion: percentage of persons from 25–29 years of age who have completed at least 4 years of college	1960 M	49†	39†	19	20
	F	26	13†	16	9†
	1970 M	58†	39†	28†	22
	F	42†	31†	50†	14†
	1976 M	60†	53†	34	34
	F	44†	35	51†	22†
5. High school overqualification: percentage of high school graduates who are employed in occupations which require less than a high school degree	1960 M	34.6†	51.8†	62.6†	40.2
	F	27.2†	44.5†	35.8	33.4†
	1970 M	33.8†	43.4†	49.3†	37.6
	F	25.7†	35.4†	33.2†	29.9†
	1976 M	43.3	48.4†	49.5†	44.2
	F	48.3	50.8†	34.8†	49.0†
6. College overqualification: percentage of persons with at least 1 year of college who are employed in occupations which typically require less education than they have	1960 M	48.2	52.4	48.1	42.7
	F	39.0	32.2†	37.1	29.8†
	1970 M	38.3†	44.3	45.1	41.7
	F	34.5†	35.0	38.2	24.7†
	1976 M	51.3†	49.4†	56.2†	44.7
	F	51.2†	41.1†	39.6	45.4
7. Earnings differential for college-educated: median earnings of those with 4 or more years of college who had some earnings during the year	1960 M	$5589	$5250	$3813	$6833
	F	487	1999	1667	1739
	1970 M	9068	10045	7793	10651
	F	1875	2171	3875	1943
	1976 M	12790	14253	13091	15165
	F	6421	8383	9038	8106

na indicates that a value was not reported due to an insufficient sample size.
†indicates that the difference between this value and the majority (male) benchmark is statistically significant at the 10 percent level.

Appendix: Identification of Needs and Recommendations, the Education of Pilipino/Pilipino-American Students*

| Source of Concern/ Recommendation | | | | | | | | Area of Concern/Needs | Recommendation(s) | **Target Population |
Security	Teachers	Counselors	Students	Community	Parents	Administrators	Researchers			
	X							ESL students' shyness may be interpreted to indicate "low ability," instead of embarrassment with language (inappropriate accent).	Increase teacher sensitivity, encourage students to "open up" and participate. Encourage students to socialize rather than isolate themselves (from both non Pilipinos and Pilipino/Pilipino-American students).	ESL

*Taken from Paula Y. Bagasao. "Educational Needs of Pilipino/Pilipino-American Junior High School Students: A Research Project." (Unpublished, Los Angeles, CA, May 30, 1980). [Editors' Note: This study reflected the issues at a particular California school.]

**GP (general population), ESL (English as a Second Language), AA/G (high achiever/gifted), A (Average student), BP/G (behavioral problem/gang)

Appendix: Identification of Needs and Recommendations (Continued)

Source of Concern/ Recommendation								Area of Concern/Needs	Recommendation(s)	**Target Population
Security	Teachers	Counselors	Students	Community	Parents	Administrators	Researchers			
	X							ESL student's shyness may be interpreted . . .	Provide teacher/counselor/ administrator inservice on cultural characteristics, student needs, and strategies.	ESL
	X			X				Students are placed in "mixed" ESL classes where there are too many different languages. The learning of proper accent (specific need of Pilipino Student) is impossible.	Provide separate ESL class (Pilipino-English).	ESL

**GP (general population), ESL (English as a Second Language), AA/G (high achiever/gifted), A (Average student), BP/G (behavioral problem/gang)

Appendix: Identification of Needs and Recommendations (Continued)

Source of Concern/Recommendation									Area of Concern/Needs	Recommendation(s)	**Target Population
Security	Teachers	Counselors	Students	Community	Parents	Administrators	Researchers				
	X		X						There are language problems in regular classes (difficulty with socializing, class participation, homework).	Increase teacher sensitivity/information. Provide Pilipino/Pilipino-American teacher aides. Allow for parent involvement in classroom instruction. Give more personalized attention.	GP, ESL
	X			X					Recent immigrants are placed by age rather than by grade in previous country (children in 7th are younger in Philippine schools).	Develop an alternative way of placing these students which accounts for differences in age/grade placements in U.S. and Philippines.	GP/ESL

**GP (general population), ESL (English as a Second Language), AA/G (high achiever/gifted), A (Average student), BP/G (behavioral problem/gang)

Appendix: Identification of Needs and Recommendations (Continued)

| Source of Concern/Recommendation | | | | | | | | Area of Concern/Needs | Recommendation(s) | **Target Population |
Security	Teachers	Counselors	Students	Community	Parents	Administrators	Researchers			
	X			X	X		X	Reinforcements/Rewards/ Motivation for "high achievers," "gifted," "highly motivated" are missing. Focus tends to be on "disadvantaged" and "problem-students." Opportunities have been limited since Proposition 13. School may be neglecting this talented ethnic group.	Examine the reward opportunities for the students (recognition award, honor rolls, etc.). Develop ways of reinforcing achievement (provide incentives, awards, etc.). Support the "image" of achievers. Develop special programs for these students (in AE program and for all students). This may involve some proposal writing for funding.	AA/G

**GP (general population), ESL (English as a Second Language), AA/G (high achiever/gifted), A (Average student), BP/G (behavioral problem/gang)

Appendix: Identification of Needs and Recommendations (Continued)

Security	Teachers	Counselors	Students	Community	Parents	Administrators	Researchers	Area of Concern/Needs	Recommendation(s)	**Target Population
								Source of Concern/Recommendation		
	X			X	X		X	Reinforcement/Rewards/. . . .	Provide advanced courses or academic opportunities in music, math, science. Provide education for professional occupations. Provide college/university exposure or early introduction.	AA/G
	X			X	X			Use of Standardized Home Language Survey does not necessarily identify language needs of Pilipino immigrant.	Make teachers aware that English may be a language of the home, but student is still in need of ESL. However, needs are specific to Pilipinos (not the same as for Hispanics, Koreans, Vietnamese).	GP/ESL

**GP (general population), ESL (English as a Second Language), AA/G (high achiever/gifted), A (Average student), BP/G (behavioral problem/gang)

Appendix: Identification of Needs and Recommendations (Continued)

Security	Teachers	Counselors	Students	Community	Parents	Administrators	Researchers	Area of Concern Needs	Recommendation(s)	**Target Population
	X		X	X	X		X	Exposure to Pilipino/Pilipino-American culture is limited. Opportunity to learn about history, language, cultural values is limited.	Infuse the teaching of Pilipino culture into regular classes (history, geography, literature etc.). Provide inservice classes or workshops to teach staff about culture and how to teach units (curriculum guides available). Offer a class in Pilipino/Pilipino-American history and culture. Offer a language class (Pilipino). Increase the number of books in the library on the Philippines and Pilipino-Americans.	GP

**GP (general population), ESL (English as a Second Language), AA/G (high achiever/gifted), A (Average student), BP/G (behavioral problem/gang)

Appendix: Identification of Needs and Recommendations (Continued)

Source of Concern/Recommendation								Area of Concern/Needs	Recommendation(s)	**Target Population
Security	Teachers	Counselors	Students	Community	Parents	Administrators	Researchers			
	X		X	X	X		X	Exposure to Pilipino/ Pilipino-American culture is limited. . . .	Increase the number of Pilipino-American staff (counselors, administrators, teachers, aides). Include Philippine music in musical productions. Provide guest speakers, role models, field trip opportunities that involve exposure to Pilipino/Pilipino-American culture. Include Philippine foods in cafeteria offerings. Attempt to get the community and parents more involved in school activities & planning.	GP

**GP (general population), ESL (English as a Second Language), AA/G (high achiever/gifted), A (Average student), BP/G (behavioral problem/gang)

Appendix: Identification of Needs and Recommendations (Continued)

Security	Teachers	Counselors	Students	Community	Parents	Administrators	Researchers	Area of Concern/Needs	Recommendation(s)	**Target Population
	X		X	X	X		X	Exposure to Pilipino/Pilipino-American culture is limited. . .	Develop a strong, lasting network and communication system between school, parents and the community	GP
				X	X		X	Average student is not readily identifiable but has unmet needs and may be subject to stereotype label of "model student" and "high achiever," which brings unfair and unrealistic expectations.	Make teachers aware of stereotypes and the effect of unfair expectations that teachers may have. Make teachers aware of individual academic and personality characteristics among this student population.	GP/A

**GP (general population), ESL (English as a Second Language), AA/G (high achiever/gifted), A (Average student), BP/G (behavioral problem/gang)

Appendix: Identification of Needs and Recommendations (Continued)

Source of Concern/Recommendation								Area of Concern/Needs	Recommendation(s)	**Target Population
Security	Teachers	Counselors	Students	Community	Parents	Administrators	Researchers			
		X						There is minimum counseling with Pilipino/Pilipino-American students (more Hispanic Students are seen).	Encourage students to talk to counselors. Counselors should realize that most of their time is focused on problem students and less on students who are cooperative.	GP
	X	X						There are problems with Parent-student relations/ parent conferences.	Provide family counseling which would learn to listen to students during school counseling sessions and how to utilize counseling services.	GP, BP/G

**GP (general population), ESL (English as a Second Language), AA/G (high achiever/gifted), A (Average student), BP/G (behavioral problem/gang)

Appendix: Identification of Needs and Recommendations (Continued)

Source of Concern/ Recommendation								Area of Concern/Needs	Recommendation(s)	**Target Population
Security	Teachers	Counselors	Students	Community	Parents	Administrators	Researchers			
	X			X			X	There are changes in types of students transferring from elementary schools to Virgil. These Pilipino/Pilipino-American students are another generation, may be less academically prepared and may create more behavior problems.	Make teachers, counselors, aware of the change characteristics. Help teachers understand the heterogeneousness of this population and the inappropriateness of "stereotyping." Create an information/communication system between elementary feeder schools and Virgil and Belmont.	GP

**GP (general population), ESL (English as a Second Language), AA/G (high achiever/gifted), A (Average student), BP/G (behavioral problem/gang)

Appendix: Identification of Needs and Recommendations (Continued)

Security	Teachers	Counselors	Students	Community	Parents	Administrators	Researchers	Area of Concern/Needs	Recommendation(s)	**Target Population
X		X						Thefts, which are the main antisocial activity, account for majority of "Busts."	Do more research on why these activities are occurring. Give more specific counseling with students involved in these activities (including parents).	BP/G
					X	X		Parents are uninformed about counseling service, PTA, advisory boards, educational opportunities, schooling process in the U.S., busing opportunities, integration issues, and student problems.	Provide workshops for parents to learn about school system and opportunities. Work for better communication with community and parents.	GP

Source of Concern/Recommendation

**GP (general population), ESL (English as a Second Language), AA/G (high achiever/gifted), A (Average student), BP/G (behavioral problem/gang)

Appendix: Identification of Needs and Recommendations (Continued)

Source of Concern/Recommendation								Area of Concern/Needs	Recommendation(s)	**Target Population
Researchers	Administrators	Parents	Community	Students	Counselors	Teachers	Security			
		X	X					There are changes in academic performance and behavior of transferees to Belmont High School (increase in truancy, tardies, dropouts; loss of interest in school work; loss of academic orientation/motivation; low rate of college attendance). This may occur at higher rates among "high achievers."	Research and document these concerns. Establish a study committee with representatives of Virgil, Belmont, community, parents. Following study, establish a committee to recommend intervention techniques.	GP
			X		X	X		Relations with parents, community, school are unsatisfactory.	Establish a community advisory committee with heavy parent involvement.	GP

**GP (general population), ESL (English as a Second Language), AA/G (high achiever/gifted), A (Average student), BP/G (behavioral problem/gang)

Appendix: Identification of Needs and Recommendations (Continued)

Source of Concern/ Recommendation								Area of Concern/Needs	Recommendation(s)	**Target Population
Security	Teachers	Counselors	Students	Community	Parents	Administrators	Researchers			
X	X	X	X	X	X			Status of gang activity in local area: is there potential for revived violence?	Make an inquiry into the presence of "Satanas," "18th Street," and other known gangs. Contacts: Youth Services Unit, Department of Community Development, County of Los Angeles; Asian Task Force, Los Angeles Police Department.	GP, BP/G
				X	X			Virgil Junior High School has "negative image." Help by members of community and parents is needed.	Establish a communication system between school, community and parents so that Virgil Junior High is better understood and properly represented.	GP

**GP (general population), ESL (English as a Second Language), AA/G (high achiever/gifted), A (Average student), BP/G (behavioral problem/gang)

Appendix: Identification of Needs and Recommendations (Continued)

Source of Concern/ Recommendation									Area of Concern/Needs	Recommendation(s)	**Target Population
Researchers	Administrators	Parents	Community	Students	Counselors	Teachers	Security			
		X	X					Virgil Junior High School	Get parents to become involved with Virgil's PTA and Advisory Board. Make the activities and opportunities of Virgil more visible to parents and community.	GP
		X	X			X		Identification of "gifted" students: are the procedures or the system of identifying "gifted" students inappropriate or biased against Pilipino/Pilipino-American students? A large number are "High Achievers," few are identified as "gifted."	Examine the procedures for identification to see if immigrants or recent arrivals are bypassed (if they were not in elementary school here). Request that teachers identify "potentially gifted" students for assessment this year.	AA/G

**GP (general population), ESL (English as a Second Language), AA/G (high achiever/gifted), A (Average student), BP/G (behavioral problem/gang)

Appendix: Identification of Needs and Recommendations (Continued)

Source of Concern/Recommendation								Area of Concern/Needs	Recommendation(s)	**Target Population
Security	Teachers	Counselors	Students	Community	Parents	Administrators	Researchers			
X		X		X				Why are "academic achievers", those who have been involved in "thefts"?	Investigate the reasons why these students who are academic achievers are acting out by "stealing." Attempt to determine if these students are attempting recognition thru antisocial behavior rather than from academic excellence; what are opportunities for academic recognition? Determine if these activities are motivated by the same factors which relate to gang membership (recognition, safety, thrills, challenge, low identity/self-concept).	BP

**GP (general population), ESL (English as a Second Language), AA/G (high achiever/gifted), A (Average student), BP/G (behavioral problem/gang)

Appendix: Identification of Needs and Recommendations (Continued)

Security	Teachers	Counselors	Students	Community	Parents	Administrators	Researchers	Area of Concern/Needs	Recommendation(s)	**Target Population
			X	X			X	Some Pilipino/Pilipino-American students are stereotyped as "model" or "ideal" students by teachers.	Inform teachers and staff of the process of stereotyping and its impact on students.	AA/G, A
			X	X	X			Ethnic intergroup relations on campus among students need improvement.	Determine if racially integrated setting means healthy student relations or if the various ethnic groups are actually segregated. Encourage interethnic communications (clubs, classes, school activities).	GP/Entire Campus

Source of Concern/Recommendation

**GP (general population), ESL (English as a Second Language), AA/G (high achiever/gifted), A (Average student), BP/G (behavioral problem/gang)

Appendix: Identification of Needs and Recommendations (Continued)

Source of Concern/Recommendation									Area of Concern/Needs	Recommendation(s)	**Target Population –
Security	Teachers	Counselors	Students	Community	Parents	Administrators	Researchers				
			X					Some Pilipino/Pilipino-American students are stereotyped as "gang members" by some Chicano students.	Provide intergroup relations workshops with various ethnic groups (included members should be student leaders from the various groups). Focus could be "stereotyping," and "labeling." One outcome of the activity should be that students realize that individual differences exist among members of one ethnic group (e.g., not all Chicanos or all Pilipinos choose to belong to gangs or clubs).	Entire Group

**GP (general population), ESL (English as a Second Language), AA/G (high   achiever/gifted) A (average student), BP/G (behavioral problem/gang)

REFERENCES

1. Marina E. Espina, "Filipinos in New Orleans," *The Proceedings of the Louisiana Academy of Science* 37 (1974): 117–21.

2. Ruben Alcantara, "Filipino Adaptation in an Hawaiian Setting" (paper presented at the Conference on International Migration for the Philippines, East-West Center, Honolulu, HI, June 2–6, 1975).

3. Belinda Aquino, "Filipino Immigrant Women in Hawaii: An Overview" (paper presented at the Sixth Annual Conference on Ethnic and Minority Studies, Institute for Minority Studies, University of Wisconsin—La Crosse, 1978).

4. Jesse Quinsaat, ed. *Letters in Exile: An Introductory Reader on the History of Pilipinos in America* (Los Angeles, CA: UCLA Asian American Studies Center, 1976).

5. Aquino.

6. Emory S. Bogardus, "Anti-Filipino Race Riots," in *Letters in Exile: An Introductory Reader on the History of Pilipinos in America,"* ed. by Jesse Quinsaat (Los Angeles, CA: UCLA Asian American Studies Center, 1976), pp. 51–62.

7. Peter C. Smith, "The Social Demography of Filipino Migrations Abroad," *International Migration Review* 10 (3) (1976): 307–53.

8. James P. Allen, "Recent Immigration from the Philippines and Filipino Communities in the United States," *The Geographical Review* 11 (1) (1977): 195–208. Detailed data on education by age group and ethnic status from the 1980 Census are not yet available. However, immigration statistics suggest that both the median years of schooling and the percent of those 25 years old and over with some college education should increase only slightly, if at all, from the 1970 data.

9. Brett H. Melendy, "California's Discrimination Against Filipinos, 1927–1935," in *Letters in Exile: An Introductory Reader on the History of Pilipinos in America,"* ed. by Jesse Quinsaat (Los Angeles, CA: UCLA Asian American Studies Center, 1976), p. 41.

10. Allen, pp. 195–208.

11. "Editorial: APAs 1970–1980," *NAAPAE Newsletter* 3 (1981): 2–5.

12. Tom Owan, *Asian-Americans: A Case of Benighted Neglect*, Occasional Paper No. 1 (Chicago, IL: Asian-American Mental Health Research Center, 1975).

13. "The Filipino Americans at a Glance," *Ningas-Cogan* 5 (10) (1976): 10–11.

14. Allen, pp. 195–208.

15. Josefina Jayme Card, "The Role of Assimilation in the Migrant Adaptation Process," in *Essays on the Filipino Experience in America,* ed. by Federico M. Macaranas. To be published.

16. Edwin B. Almirol, *A Study of Paradoxes: Filipino American Economic Conditions* (Davis, CA: University of California at Davis, 1980).

17. Monica Boyd, "The Changing Nature of Central and Southeast Asian Immigration to the United States: 1961–1972," *International Migration Review* 8 (4) (1974): 507–520.

18. U.S. Department of Justice, Annual Reports to the Immigration and Naturalization Service, 1975, pp. 44–52, . . . 1976, pp. 44–56; . . . 1977, pp. 38–47; . . . 1979, pp. 16–19. Washington, DC: U.S. Government Printing Office.

19. Federico M. Macaranas, "Potential Problems of the Filipino Youth" (paper presented at the Conference on Asian Americans: Agenda for Action, New York State Advisory Committee to the U.S. Commission on Civil Rights, New York, NY, May 6, 1978).

20. Urban Associates, Inc., *A Study of Selected Socio-economic Characteristics of Ethnic Minorities Based on the 1970 Census, Vol. II: Asian Americans* (Washington, DC: U.S. Government Printing Office, HEW Publication No. (OS) 75-121, 1974).

21. Federico M. Macaranas, *Education and Income Inequality: The Case of Young Filipino Americans* (New York: School of Business Research Institute, Manhattan College, 1978), pp. 8–10.

22. Mary Ayupan and Gary N. Howells, *A Multiple Regression Analysis of College Attendance among Pilipino Males and Pilipino Females in California* (Stockton, CA: University of the Pacific, 1980); Peter Chi, "Inter- and Intra-Group Inequalities of the Racial and Ethnic Groups in the United States (Ph.D. diss., Brown University, 1972); Gary N. Howells and Isabelita B. Sarabia, "Education of the Pilipino Child," *Integrated Education* 16 (2) (1978):17–20; and Juanita Tamayo Lott, "An Attempt," in *Diwang Pilipino*, ed. by J. Navarro (Davis, CA: University of California at Davis, 1974), pp. 3–14.

23. R.F. Flor, "Filipino Experience and Education," in *Know Yourself, Penoy: An Introduction to the Filipino-American Experience* ed. by Ben Menor (Santa Cruz, CA: Third World Resource Teaching Center, University of California, 1975); Lott, "An Attempt," pp. 3–14; and Juanita Tamayo Lott, "Migration of a Mentality: The Pilipino Community," *Social Casework* 57 (3) (March 1976): 165–72.

24. Lott, "An Attempt," p. 10.

25. Melendy, p. 37.

26. Carlos Bulosan, *America Is in the Heart* (New York: Harcourt, Brace and Company, 1946).

27. The World Bank, "The Education System," in *The Philippines: Priorities and Prospects for Development* (Washington, DC: The World Bank, 1976), p. 291.

28. Macaranas, *Education and Income Inequality.* . . .

29. Samuel Bowles and Herbert Gintis, *Schooling in Capitalist America: Educational Reform and the Contradictions of Economic Life* (New York: Basic Books, 1976).

30. Robert J. Havighurst and Bernice L. Neugarten, *Society and Education*, 4th ed. (Boston: Allyn and Bacon, Inc., 1975), pp. 26–31.

31. Bienvenido D. Junasa, "Study of Some Social Factors Related to the Plans and Aspiration of the Filipino Youth in Waipahu" (Master's thesis, University of Hawaii, 1961).

32. Almirol (see note 16); Amado Y. Cabezas and H. Yee, *Discriminatory Employment of Asian-Americans, Private Industry in the San Francisco-Oakland SMSA* (San Francisco, CA: ASIAN, Inc., 1977); Lirio S. Covey, "An Evaluation of Discrimination Against Filipinos in the Resume-Review Phase of the Job Selection Process" (paper presented at the Conference on the Filipino Experience in America, The Asia Society, New York, NY, March, 1977); and Angelina Li, "Labor Utilization and the Assimilation of Asian Americans" (Report prepared for the Employment and Training Administration, Department of Labor, University of Chicago, Chicago, IL, June 1980).

33. Shirley Hune, *Pacific Migration to the United States: Trends and Themes in Historical and Sociological Literature* (Washington, DC: Research Institute on Immigration and Ethnic Studies, Smithsonian Institute, 1977), p. 43.

34. Marcaranas, *Education and Income Inequality.* . . .

35. Chi, p. 121.

36. Barry R. Chiswick, "The Effect of Americanization on the Earnings of Foreign-Born Men," *Journal of Political Economy* 86 (1978): 897–922; and Edwin Fujii and James Mak, "The Relative Economic Progress of Hawaii-Born and Immigrant Filipino Men in Hawaii" (paper presented at the Second International Conference on Philippine Studies, Honolulu, HI, June 26–30, 1981).

37. Sixto Roxas, "Financing Private Education in the Philippines," in *Philippine Education: A Forward Look*, ed. by Miguel B. Gaffud and Aurelio O. Elevazo (Manila, Philippines: First National Conference on Education, 1965), pp. 92–93.

38. The World Bank, p. 292.

39. Marcaranas, *Education and Income Inequality. . . .*

40. Ayupan and Howells.

41. Ayupan and Howells, p. 12.

42. Macaranas, *Education and Income Inequality. . . .*; and U.S. Commission on Civil Rights, *Social Indicators of Equality for Minorities* (Washington, DC: U.S. Government Printing Office, 1978); and Urban Associates, Inc.

43. Fujii and Mak, p. 29.

44. Fujii and Mak, p. 33.

45. Barry R. Chiswick, "Earnings and Employment among Asian-American Men," (paper presented at the Second International Conference on Philippine Studies, Honolulu, HI, June 26–30, 1981).

46. Chiswick, "Earnings and Employment among Asian-American Men," p. 11.

47. National Commission on Manpower Policy, *From School to Work: Improving the Transition* (Washington, DC: U.S. Government Printing Office, 1976), pp. 90–96; 168–70.

48. Paula Y. Bagasao, "Educational Needs of Pilipino/Pilipino-American Junior High School Students: A Research Project" (Unpublished, Los Angeles, CA, May 30, 1980).

49. The World Bank, p. 287.

50. Bagasao, p. 17.

51. Amefil Agbayani, "Political Definitions in Research and Educational Programs that Affect Immigrant Children in Hawaii," (paper presented at the First National Conference of the National Association of Asian and Pacific American Education, San Francisco, CA, April, 1979).

52. Agbayani.

53. Hune, p. 22–42.

54. Juanita S. Burris, "Childrearing Values and Concerns of Filipino Parents: The View from Chicago" (paper presented at the Conference on the Filipino Experience in America, 29th Annual Meeting of the Association for Asian Studies, New York, NY, March, 1977); and Card, in *Essays on the Filipino Experience in America.*

55. Donald T. Mizokawa and James K. Morishima, "The Education for, by and of Asian/Pacific-Americans," *Research Review of Equal Education* 3 (3) (1979), pp. 3–33.

56. Patricia M. Arias, "Factors in Counseling the Filipino Student" (Master's thesis, California State University at Hayward, 1973); E.P. Dagot, "The Cultural and Linguistic Features in Cross-Cultural Communication Between Filipino Students and Americans and the Use of the Short Story to Teach These Features" (Ed.D. diss., New York University, 1967); Joselito W. Lalas, "The Cueing Strategies Used by Filipino Bilingual Students in Reading" (Master's in Education project, Seattle Pacific University, 1979); Patricia Le Vasseur, "Identity Patterns among Pilipino-American Youths" (Master's thesis, University of California at Berkeley, 1973); Federico K. Maglangit, "The English Pronunciation Problem of the Native Maranao Speaker" (Master's thesis, Cornell University, 1954); Domingo F. Nolasco, "A Study of Filipino Graduates in California High Schools" (Master's thesis, University of California at Berkeley, 1933); Salud A. Ortega, "The English Pronunciation Problems of the Native Speaker of Tagalog" (Master's thesis, Cornell University, 1955); Annie Respicio-Diaz, "Factors Associated with Choice of Major in Science Among Filipino Students" (Ph.D. diss., George Washington University, 1968); Albert Reyes, "Interpersonal Behavior Patterns of Filipino-American College Students" (Master's thesis, California State University at Hayward, 1973); and Milagros R. Romaquin, "Filipino Aural-Oral Discrimination of Selected English Words" (Master's thesis, University of California at Los Angeles, 1965).

57. G. Baltazar et al., "A Manual for Non-Filipino Teachers Working with Filipino Children" (Unpublished Manuscript, University of the Pacific, 1977); Socorro Espiritu, "A Study of the Treatment of the Philippines in Selected Social Studies Textbooks Published in the U.S. for Use in the Elementary and Secondary Schools" (Ph.D. diss., Syracuse University, 1954); and C.Y. Yu, "Pilipino Educators vs. Textbook Publishers in California," *Interracial Books for Children Bulletin* 8 (2) (1977): 6–8.

SELECTED BIBLIOGRAPHY

Aldana, Benigno. *The Education System of the Philippines*. Manila, Philippines: University Publishing Company, 1949.

Cabezas, Amado Y. "A View of Poor Linkage between Education, Occupation and Earnings of Asian Americans." Paper presented at the Third National Forum on Education and Work, San Francisco, CA, 1977.

Callao, Maximo Jose. "Culture Shock—West, East and West Again," *Personnel and Guidance Journal* 51 (February 1973): 413–16.

Cerenia, Virginia R., and Lum, John B. "Some Current Classroom Practices in Asian Bilingual Education: Research Considerations and Conceptualizations." Unpublished paper.

Cordova, Fred. "The Filipino-American: There's Always an Identity Crisis," in *Asian American Psychological Perspectives*, edited by Stanley Sue and Nathaniel Wagner. Palo Alto, CA: Science and Behavior Books, Inc., 1973.

Galang, Rosita G. "Research Findings on Bilingualism and Bilingual Education in the Philippines: Implications for Instruction in the Filipino American Bilingual Classroom." Paper presented at the First National Conference of the National Association for Asian and Pacific American Education, San Francisco, CA, April, 1979.

Macaranas, Federico M. "Education and Income Inequality Among Asian Americans." Paper presented at the First National Conference of the National Association for Asian and Pacific American Education, San Francisco, CA, April, 1979.

———. "Social Indicators of Education and the Model Minority Thesis." Paper presented at the Second National Conference of the National Association for Asian Pacific American Education, Washington, DC, April, 1980.

Menor, Ben Jr., ed., *Know Yourself, Pinoy: An Introduction to the Filipino-American Experience*. Santa Cruz, CA: Third World Teaching Resource Center, University of California, 1975.

National Center for Education Statistics, U.S. Department of Health, Education and Welfare. "Birthplace and Language Characteristics of Persons of Chinese, Japanese, Korean, Filipino, and Vietnamese Origin in the United States, Spring 1976." *NCES Bulletin* (79 B-12) (May 21, 1979): 79–144.

Navarro, J., ed. *Diwang Pilipino*. Davis, CA: University of California, 1974.

Quinsaat, Jesse, ed. *Letters in Exile: An Introductory Reader on the History of Pilipinos in America*. Los Angeles, CA: UCLA Asian American Studies Center, 1976.

Ramos, Teresita V. "Bilingual Education and Public Policy in Hawaii: Historical and Current Issues." Paper presented at the First National Conference of the National Association for Asian and Pacific American Education, San Francisco, CA, April, 1979.

Sowell, Thomas, ed. *Essays and Data on American Ethnic Groups* (Washington, DC: The Urban Institute, 1979.

The Indochinese in America: Who Are They and How Are They Doing?

by Vuong G. Thuy

This paper is a modest attempt to look at different aspects of the immigration of the Indochinese to the United States from 1975 to the present time. In addition, the problems and progress in the resettlement of these new Americans will be examined from a cross-cultural perspective. The paper will focus on their linguistic, ethnic, cultural, and educational characteristics. It will also examine the implementation of federal, state, and local policies and programs designed to assist Indochinese refugees.

After a long and frustrating search for data and materials dealing with these new immigrants, the author is led to believe that, so far, the study of the migration and resettlement of the Indochinese refugees has been quite limited. Such studies have probably been impeded not only by the lack of interest in research on the part of governmental and voluntary agencies, but also by the lack of resources available to scholars and researchers, particularly those who are Indochinese. Although scholarly studies on the backgrounds, migration, adjustment problems, and progress of the refugees are scarce, quite a few piecemeal, unpublished materials dealing with the Indochinese refugees in the U.S. do exist. By and large, these unpublished materials are accurate, written by Indochinese educators and/or social workers who saw an urgent need to write such materials in order to help their non-Indochinese colleagues, the American public, and sponsors of Indochinese refugees to understand them.[1] Interestingly, the few available scholarly studies on these refugees were mostly written by non-Indochinese scholars and researchers.

HISTORICAL BACKGROUND

The fall of Saigon in April 1975 triggered an abrupt and mass exodus of refugees from Indochina to the United States, beginning with the controversial "baby lift" which brought 2,643 orphans to the U.S. from orphanages in Vietnam. (Some of these children were alleged to be not orphans, but instead children of influential Vietnamese and/or Vietnamese who worked with the Americans in Vietnam.) Within the days before and after the collapse of the American-supported regime in South Vietnam, approximately 145,000 Indochinese refugees—the majority of whom were Vietnamese associated with the war effort in Vietnam—were evacuated to the U.S. This was the beginning of a new and dramatic chapter in the migration history of the United States. Also among these first Indochinese refugees were a small number of Laotians, Hmong tribespeople of Laos, and Cambodians.

More than 7 years later, the traumatic migration of refugees from Indochina has still not ceased. On the contrary, refugees from Indochina continue to arrive in refugee camps in Southeast Asia. Hundreds of thousands of Vietnamese have fled their homeland in small and unseaworthy crafts to seek asylum in neighboring countries, with the hope of eventually being resettled in the U.S. or Third World countries. Thousands of Laotians have swum the Mekong River to Thailand, seeking freedom and a new life; numerous Cambodians have also risked their lives by fleeing through mined jungles into Thailand to look for freedom and a new beginning. Despite the horrible conditions in refugee camps and unbelievable personal suffering during their freedom flight, many uprooted Indochinese continue to arrive in refugee camps, in some cases leaving behind loved ones and worrying about their safety and welfare in their homelands. As many as 40 percent of the fleeing refugees are believed to have perished.

For convenience's sake, and in order to better describe the makeup of the refugees, the exodus of the Indochinese refugees from 1975 to the present time can be arbitrarily divided into 2 major waves of migration: (1) the first wave, who arrived in the U.S. in 1975 and 1976 directly from Vietnam, Laos, and Cambodia through refugee reception centers at Guam; Wake Island; Subic Bay, Philippines; Camp Pendleton, California; Camp Fort Chaffe, Arkansas; Eglin Airforce Base, Florida; and Fort Indiantown Gap, Pennsylvania; and (2) the second wave, who have arrived in the U.S. from 1976 to the present. These refugees have not come directly from Indochina, but rather from refugee camps in Thailand, Malaysia, Hongkong, Macau, Indonesia, the Philippines, Singapore, Japan, Korea, and

Taiwan. By and large, the second wave has included: the Laotian refugees and the Hmong tribespeople of Laos who crossed the Mekong River to Thailand; the Cambodian refugees who escaped famine and the war in Cambodia to enter Thailand; and the Vietnamese and Chinese Vietnamese who set sail from their homeland to seek asylum in refugee camps and who have been known as "the boat people."

DEMOGRAPHIC AND ETHNIC PROFILES

Prior to the arrival of the first Indochinese refugees on American soil, the Indochinese colony in the U.S.—composed primarily of Vietnamese—numbered fewer than 10,000. The largest concentration (a few thousand) was in the greater Washington, DC area. The other Indochinese were scattered throughout the U.S. and included immigrants, clergymen, and sojourners, such as students, short-term trainees, and diplomats.

According to the March 26, 1982 issue of the *Refugee Report*, the total Indochinese refugee population in the U.S. as of January 1982 was 573,328, distributed unequally in the 50 states of the Union and U.S. Territories (Virgin Islands, Guam, and Puerto Rico).[2] California ranked first with 193,841 refugees, followed by Texas with 51,932, and Washington (state) with 26,602. The 3 states having the lowest concentrations of refugees were Delaware with 297 refugees, Vermont with 301 and New Hampshire with 395. Table 1 (page 108) gives a better illustration of the distribution of Indochinese refugees in the U.S.

Furthermore, the statistical reports of the Office of Refugee Affairs, U.S. Department of State, showed that the Indochinese refugee population in Southeast Asia as of November, 1981 was 261,238.

Based on the resettlement patterns of Indochinese refugees in the past 6 years, one is led to believe that the newly arrived refugees will tend to settle in urban areas with large concentrations of refugees, such as Southern California, Houston, Dallas, New Orleans, Seattle, and greater Washington, DC. The newly arrived refugees usually wish to be reunited with relatives or friends who came to the U.S. before them, indicating that the locations or states which already have large concentrations of refugees will continue to receive more refugees. One does not forget that the federal agencies responsible for the resettlement of Indochinese refugees allegedly adopted a policy of dispersing the refugees over all the 50 states, including sparsely populated states such as Alaska. Regardless of whatever the cited reasons might have been, however, this short-sighted policy did not take into consideration the real needs of the refugees and was largely responsible for the secondary interstate migration, apparent as early as the beginning of 1976. After a fairly short period of resettlement, many refugees left their first or even second place of resettlement to regroup in ethnic clusters found in Florida, Louisiana, Texas, Washington, DC, and particularly California. They left everything behind to start all over again where they felt "at home" among their own people. Other motivations for secondary or tertiary migration included the warm weather; better opportunities for job training; employment and education; and a desire to be close to relatives, friends and compatriots. Another moving force was that, when many refugees ventured out of their ethnic shells to explore their new and alien world and surroundings, they met with alienation and in some cases ugly hostility, which forced many to withdraw into their ethnic enclaves for protection and comfort and slowed their acculturation. The secondary or tertiary migration not only brought about damaging economic, emotional, and psychological consequences for a good number of affected refugees, it also created frustration and disappointment for the refugees, their American sponsors, and all those who had tried hard to help the refugees adjust to American life. It is important to note, however, that, although a number of refugees experienced some sort of hostility, the Indochinese refugees by and large did not encounter the kind of racial discrimination and physical violence experienced by their Asian predecessors, namely the Japanese and Chinese Americans.

From 1975 to 1976, 42 percent of roughly 150,000 refugees from the first wave were under 18 years of age; thus, approximately 65,000 refugees were of school age. The unexpected and sudden appearance of this substantial school age population in the public schools led to serious problems and caused a severe impact on a number of schools in places such as Southern California and Texas where there were large concentrations of refugees. American unfamiliarity with the Indochinese languages, cultures, and educational systems aggravated the problems.

In the first wave, 62 percent of the refugees arrived in family groups of 5 or more persons. It is interesting to note that 2,118 of these large families, accounting for a total of 14,811 refugees, had a woman as the head of the household. This wave of refugees was generally ethnically and linguistically more homogeneous than the second wave and consisted mainly of Vietnamese. Two-thirds of these refugees were quite urbanized. Before their arrival in the United States, a good number of them were not only already well-educated and from well-to-do families by Vietnamese standards, they also had been exposed to Western culture and the English language, due to the French occupation and American involvement in Vietnam. Many were professionals and/or members of the educational and social elite, and, generally speaking, they had occupied relatively high economic statuses in their native country.

The second wave of refugees has been much more heterogeneous in terms of their linguistic, cultural, geographic, and educational backgrounds. The major groups of refugees in this wave have been Vietnamese, Chinese Vietnamese (from both North and South Vietnam), Cambodians, Laotians, and the Hmong tribespeople of Laos. Compared to the refugees of the first wave, the refugees of the second wave have included more males (57.6 percent compared to 54.7 percent) and fewer older men and women. Many second wave males have been single or have arrived in the U.S. without their wives and/or children, partly because of the well-publicized attacks and barbarianism of Thai pirates and partly because of the hardship and high cost of the escape. Available data show only a slightly higher proportion of children among the newer refugees (44.5 percent age 0–17 years compared to 42.6 percent in the first wave) and a higher proportion of working persons (47.7 percent compared to 45.6 percent).

Although statistical data on the educational, occupational, and socioeconomic background of the second wave refugees are not available, observations, feedback, and personal experience all indicate that, generally, these refugees have come to the U.S. in poor health, with much lower educational and socioeconomic backgrounds, and with fewer marketable skills than their predecessors. They have also seemed to have less capability in the English language and little or no exposure to Western culture and urban living. A substantial number of them have been semiilliterate or illiterate. As such, and according to past experiences, the resettlement, acculturation, and education of the new refugees will likely be more time consuming and require more efforts and resources.

Of the total Indochinese refugee population already in the U.S., roughly 85 percent are Vietnamese (including a small number of Chinese Vietnamese), 10 percent are Laotians (including Hmong), and 5 percent are Cambodians. It should be noted that a majority of the Chinese-Vietnamese refugees came in the second wave. Indochinese-American ethnic makeup is gradually changing because of the steady influx of Cambodian refugees to the U.S. and the decreased admission of Vietnamese refugees.

The flow of refugees during 1979 included a number of unaccompanied minors, mostly teenage boys. Between March 1 and September 30, 1979, 423 unaccompanied minors from Indochina were reportedly resettled in 11 states. It is not clear, however, whether this figure includes any of the 400 or so unaccompanied minors between the ages of 2 and 16 who were reported to have been evacuated from Vietnam in the 1975 Baby Lift.[3] (For a variety of unclear reasons, it seems that many of the baby lift orphans and unaccompanied minors were deliberately dispersed culturally by being placed with majority White families, instead of Indochinese or Asian families.)

TABLE 1: Current Indochinese Refugee Population in the U.S. by State as of January 1982[4]

State	Total	State	Total
Alabama	2,442	Nevada	2,296
Alaska	461	New Hampshire	395
Arizona	3,834	New Jersey	5,174
Arkansas	2,631	New Mexico	2,988
California	193,841	New York	17,550
Colorado	9,153	North Carolina	4,670
Connecticut	5,385	North Dakota	648
Delaware	297	Ohio	7,428
District of Columbia	2,000	Oklahoma	7,320
Florida	10,039	Oregon	16,707
Georgia	6,724	Pennsylvania	21,748
Hawaii	6,309	Rhode Island	3,529
Idaho	1,211	South Carolina	2,155
Illinois	21,670	South Dakota	903
Indiana	3,959	Tennessee	3,393
Iowa	8,412	Texas	51,932
Kansas	7,865	Utah	7,287
Kentucky	2,094	Vermont	301
Louisiana	12,922	Virginia	16,949
Maine	1,004	Washington	26,602
Maryland	6,209	West Virginia	474
Massachusetts	11,372	Wisconsin	9,775
Michigan	9,308	Wyoming	424
Minnesota	23,238	Guam	328
Mississippi	1,572	Puerto Rico	25
Missouri	5,337	Virgin Islands	16
Montana	1,013	Other	6
Nebraska	2,003	Unknown	0
		TOTAL	573,328

THE EFFECTS OF RESETTLEMENT ON INDOCHINESE REFUGEES

With the background described above, one could almost predict the Indochinese resettlement problems from the outset. The arrival of the first refugees in 1975 caught the American public, and especially those who would be responsible for their resettlement, off guard. The unpreparedness of American sponsors, educators, social workers, and other service providers led to untold frustration, concern, and sometimes anger. In addition to the tremendous culture shock brought about by the vast and obvious cultural differences, the Indochinese refugees (of both waves) had to face a host of obstacles and/or problems in their efforts to resettle in their new country. Their unfamiliarity with the English language and the American way of life, coupled with a lack of knowledge about the legal, economic, transportation, and social service systems, frustrated and alienated them and hampered their resettlement. Their language deficiencies and lack of marketable and/or required skills often resulted in unemployment, underemployment or employment in low paying, menial jobs. Many refugee families of 6 or more persons faced serious housing problems. Housing codes, together with employment pressures and/or employment training needs, adversely affected the refugees' traditional child rearing practices and family life styles, which are characterized by eating habits and sleeping patterns which are very different from those of Americans. Resettlement efforts for women with children substantially reduced the amount of time that they were usually able to spend at home taking care of family members. For a good number of Indochinese mothers, inadequate or unavailable child care has not allowed them or has made it difficult for them to attend English classes and/or to participate in job training programs so that they are able to seek employment and get off the public assistance rolls.

The loss of status as the sole breadwinners and authority figures of the family has saddened and psychologically depressed a good number of male heads of Indochinese refugee families. Furthermore, the role change created by the acute need for Indochinese housewives to go out and work instead of remaining economically dependent has sometimes strained marital relationships, and added to the seemingly unbearable problems facing many Indochinese male refugees. In a number of cases, marital problems have reportedly resulted in divorce, considered unusual in Indochinese culture.

New and low social and economic status caused by unemployment, underemployment, or low paying, menial jobs has left ugly psychological scars on many male refugees. Being unable to cope with the culture shock and multifaceted resettlement problems, some have reportedly taken or have tried to take their own lives and in some cases the lives of family members. Mental health problems, therefore, have increased and/or are surfacing among a number of refugees. Especially troubled have been those who have left their spouses and/or children in their homelands; these refugees continue to suffer from feelings of guilt. The male refugees who were in authoritative positions and/or enjoyed a high social, economic, and prestige status in their native countries tend to live in their pasts as an escape from the hard and cruel realities of the present, thus endangering or aggravating their mental health. Furthermore, Western ways of treating mental health problems do not seem to work well for Indochinese refugees; poor communication between American psychiatrists and Indochinese patients and cultural differences are among the reasons for this failure. The mental health problems described above—such as feelings of guilt, depression, anxiety, alienation in the new culture, and sadness because of loss of country, property and status—have been common and are still found among refugees. And, these problems have impeded refugee resettlement.

Practices which are quite acceptable in American culture, and the values which are taught and observed in American schools, sometimes collide head-on with those which are taught and observed in Indochinese families. American cultural practices and beliefs such as dating and reverence of individuality are 2 possible sources of conflict between Indochinese school children and their parents. This often leads to family disturbances and discord, and, in turn, strains the parent-child relationship and widens the generation gap. In addition, the practice of placement by age rather than academic preparation makes education in American schools irrelevant, inappropriate, and inequitable for a significant number of refugee children who are older and/or have received limited or no education in their homelands. Placement problems have led to a high drop-out rate among illiterate and semiilliterate children, older children, or children with limited past education because, in addition to the tremendous language barrier and unfamiliarity with the American educational system, these children are unable to live up to the academic expectations of the teacher. Furthermore, the absence of bilingual teachers and linguistically relevant materials has further exacerbated the educational problems of refugees.

The sudden influx of this new refugee population has created serious concerns in terms of educational services and resources. Confronted with the seemingly impossible task of educating foreign-born children whose cultural, linguistic, and educational backgrounds they knew very little about, many teachers and school administrators have reportedly become frustrated, or even angry, and have cried for help. To educate Indochinese refugees has been a real challenge for American educators. But challenges need not be negative. If they are handled properly, they can be quite positive. Nevertheless, a bright side of this seemingly difficult situation has been that the personal efforts and willingness of American educators to teach Indochinese children of the first wave has prepared teachers and administrators to work more effectively with the newer Indochinese refugee children. Ironically, because of the current trend of decreasing enrollment in our public schools, the influx of Indochinese refugee children has even been considered a blessing by some school administrators and teachers. Allegedly, a number of classroom teachers have tried to get these well-disciplined and highly motivated students from Indochina into their classrooms. Some have even gone as far as "hiding" these students by keeping them away from such special services as bilingual and English as a second language (ESL) instruction, services these students need badly.

Although published research and data are minimal at this point, more than 7 years after their arrival, the refugees of the first wave seem to be doing quite well, taking into consideration their foreign educational and different socioeconomic backgrounds. The majority of them have resettled in material comfort and are self-sufficient, if not prospering. A good number of refugee families now have a TV (if not a color TV), one or two cars, and one or even two houses. Many of them hold 2 jobs in order to support their large families and have unquestionably become contributing members of this pluralistic society.

Indochinese refugees reportedly paid no less than 29 million dollars in taxes to the U.S. Treasury in 1979 and more than 80 million dollars in 1980, thus clearly dismissing the unfounded fear that they would unduly overburden America's public assistance rolls and set up ghettoes in American cities. Furthermore, despite the language barrier and unfamiliarity with the American educational system, many Indochinese children with a grade-level education similar to their American peers, and especially the young ones, have performed quite well in school. It is no longer rare to come across students with Indochinese names on the honor rolls of American schools or in the best known universities in the country.

Because of past experiences in their homelands and refugee camps, the newer refugees seem to face more problems in their resettlement than their predecessors did. In addition, the trauma of their freedom flights and extended stays in refugee camps have created numerous health, mental, and psychological problems which makes their resettlement and mainstreaming more difficult and time consuming. Malnutrition and the not-long-ago famine in Cambodia may have also severely affected the learning abilities of a number of children from Cambodia, who will need special attention and help from American bilingual teachers, monolingual teachers, and school administrators. In order to facilitate the mainstreaming of the recent refugee children, public funds will be needed to purchase appropriate materials, hire bilingual teachers, and provide cross-cultural, linguistic, and professional training to American educators. The placement and education of these children calls for special patience and understanding on the part of parents, school administrators, and teachers alike, because a substantial number of school-age children from Indochina not only face language problems and are unfamiliar with the American educational system, but they have also lost a good deal of study time in their native countries and in refugee camps. Another problem for students has been the loss of diplomas, transcripts, and/or school records. Because of these problems, new Indochinese students have felt threatened, alienated, frightened, and uneasy.

The acquisition of the English language is, of course, ranked first among refugees' priorities. At this state, a bilingual program or a heavy dose of English as a second language, preferably administered by bilingual personnel, is a wise move. Since there is a very little in common linguistically between English and the various Indochinese languages, learning the English language can be a frustrating experience for students and teachers alike. The problem is worsened if the student has had limited or no exposure to the English language and the American culture prior to resettlement. If the student is not placed at his/her appropriate level, or if s/he is placed in an ESL class with many different levels (as is usually the case), the experience can be quite traumatic. The student will encounter numerous difficulties with English phonology, morphology, and syntax. English pronunciation, intonation, vowels, consonants, and particularly clusters of more than 2 consonants are a few of the serious learning problems created for Indochinese students. Futhermore, the inconsistencies and irregularities in terms of spelling, word formation, and grammatical structures of the English language will frustrate and discourage these students as well as slow down their language acquisition. Although illiteracy or semiilliteracy in their native language will augment the problem for many Indochinese students, the natural bilingual and bicultural background of a number of them, especially the ethnic Chinese, will help them acquire the English language and mainstream into the American classroom and society more easily and quickly. In addition, their peculiar learning styles, such as rote learning and passive classroom behavior (as a manifestation of respect for the teacher) may bewilder, and be misinterpreted by, the American teacher. Finally, the racial prejudices and jealousy expressed overtly or covertly by some majority and other ethnic minority students in the school may cause students from Indochina to form and stick to their own groups for self-protection against hostility and occasional physical abuses. The formation of ethnic cliques will inevitably hinder their mainstreaming, interfere with the learning process, and create conflicts between Indochinese students and other students at school.

The above problems are the foundation for the difficulties affecting the mainstreaming of the newly arrived refugee child. His/her total educational experience will depend on the formal process of instruction and the informal interactions in the school and will influence and eventually shape the child's attitudes, cognition, and perception about him/herself and others throughout his/her life. Therefore, a quality integrated educational program is certainly a necessity to ensure the maximum growth for the child and to prepare him/her to live in this multicultural society. Since the desegregation-integration process is a very complex one and is heavily influenced if not determined by internal and external forces, one has to be aware of how this process works. One of the most important components of the process is the understanding and appreciation of not only cross-cultural differences, but also the contributions of culturally different members to this pluralistic society.

THE LAW AND THE RESETTLEMENT OF REFUGEES

To deal with the mass and sudden migration of refugees from Indochina, on May 22, 1975, a joint House and Senate conference committee agreed on the final language of the Indochina Migration and Refugee Assistance Act of 1975, which appropriated $405,000,000 for the administration's refugee program. Two days later, the act became P.L. 94-23 when President Ford signed it into law. The migration and resettlement rights of Indochinese refugees were thus protected and facilitated, and public funds were appropriated for different aspects of resettlement. In addition to P.L. 94-23, the Indochina Refugee Children Assistance Act of 1976 (P.L. 94-405) (later amended by P.L. 95-561) provided public funds for the education of elementary-secondary students. Furthermore, the U.S. Congress continued to provide temporary authority and funding for the resettlement program (from employment and language training to mental health) through a series of 5 pieces of legislation: P.L. 95-145, P.L. 95-549, P.L. 96-86, P.L. 96-110, and P.L. 96-123. Due to a lack of strict rules and regulations and the fact that Indochinese educators and parents were not allowed to participate in the decision-making process and program administration, public money provided by the Indochina Refugee Children

Assistance Act for the education of refugees did not seem to work effectively. Local educational agencies, which received these funds through state educational agencies on the basis of the number of enrolled students, were given almost total freedom to spend the money as they pleased and for the purposes and the target populations they deemed important. In some isolated cases, the situation was worsened when the Indochinese educational funds were administered by other minorities who allegedly seemed to be more interested in serving the members of their groups rather than Indochinese students.

In March 1979, the Carter Administration proposed new legislation to the U.S. Congress to provide a comprehensive and permanent statutory authority regarding the establishment of regular procedures for determining the number of refugees to be admitted to the United States and the establishment of equitable assistance and service programs for all refugees accepted by this country, regardless of country of origin. On March 17, 1980 the administration's proposed Refugee Act of 1979 became P.L. 96-212 and known as the Refugee Act of 1980. As such, this act brought to an end the period of piecemeal legislation for refugees.

Unlike their Chinese and Japanese predecessors who came to this country in the early twentieth century without legislation to protect and assist them (and who were exposed to blatant racial discrimination, severe hostility, and sometimes cruel treatment), the more recent Indochinese refugees have generally enjoyed the protection, assistance, and hospitality of the American people and government. This assistance has been manifested by legislation and by the very fact that so many American citizens, church groups, and organizations have been willing to sponsor Indochinese refugees. Although there have been some occasional hostilities and ugly encounters due primarily to misunderstanding and misinformation, and despite the fact that the refugees came at a time of economic depression and high unemployment (nearly 9 percent), a large proportion of the American people not only welcomed, but also were eager to assist Indochinese refugees. In fact, in the history of immigration in the United States, seldom has one noticed the kind of emotional ties which are commonly found among Indochinese refugees and their American sponsors.

THE FUTURE OF THE INDOCHINESE REFUGEES

Although the physical resettlement of the refugees of the first wave can be said to have been relatively smooth and without major crises, cultural and linguistic differences, coupled with discrimination and unfamiliar practices in the U.S., have often made refugee adjustment to American society painful.

And yet, according to all indications, the refugees of the first wave generally seem to have made substantial economic progress in a short period of time and have become self-sufficient. There are signs that the hard working Indochinese refugees, or at least those who came to the United States during the first wave, will not only "make it" but will also do well in their adoptive country in no time. Although up-to-date data are not available yet, the Social Security Index, which records the number of persons aged 20–59 who receive earnings in jobs covered by Social Security, indicates that already in 1977 (or just 2 years after their arrival in the U.S.), 90 percent of male refugees and 61.2 percent of female refugees received earnings comparable to 93 percent of male Americans and 63.5 percent of female Americans of the total population.

The success story of the earlier refugees, however, should not blur or cover the special needs and problems of the newly arrived refugees, nor should it overshadow the problems the refugees from Indochina in general are still facing in the American pluralistic society. In addition to the current economic ills—inflation and high unemployment—the visibility and success of the earlier refugees have led to increased hostility from other minorities as well as the majority in some confined areas of the United States. The number of racial incidents and/or economic competitions, mainly due to misunderstanding and misinformation, has reportedly increased in places with large concentrations of Indochinese refugees. Regrettable incidents and dangerous confrontations such as those in the Southern part of Texas and Denver, Colorado have been widely covered by the media. Similarly, racial encounters are imminent in places such as Southern California. They may prove to be explosive if nothing is done to defuse them.

Due to an acute lack of information and contracts between members of different ethnic groups, some members of other minority groups, through rumors, or because of pure jealousy, have been led to believe wrongly that Indochinese refugees have been receiving preferential treatment in terms of housing, public assistance, and other social services. Adding to the problem, a good number of refugees still do not understand, nor are aware of, local mores, taboos, customs, traditions, values, expectations, and practices in the U.S. In addition to the much-needed informal contacts and exchange of information between different ethnic communities, orientation programs for the leaders and members of these communities, especially for Indochinese refugees, must be set up immediately. These programs should be funded by federal, state, local, and voluntary agencies responsible for the resettlement of refugees; and they should be conducted by qualified members of various ethnic groups, with the aim of reducing imminent racial tensions. In this author's book, entitled *Getting to Know the Vietnamese and Their Culture* (1976), orientation programs for both Indochinese refugees members of other ethnic groups, including the majority group, were suggested. However, little or nothing has been done in this crucial area. According to the practice so far, once a refugee is sponsored, the voluntary agency in charge will dump him/her into society without any follow-up, and force him/her to "sink or swim."

In addition to existing hostilities, a number of refugees, including the earlier refugees, still face underemployment, unemployment, and a host of other resettlement problems such as culture shock, the English language barrier, and a sense of guilt, depression, alienation, discrimination and loneliness. In a way, the newer refugees from Indochina are more fortunate then their predecessors because, upon arriving in the U.S., they immediately found, in their relatives and/or the members of their existing ethnic community, the financial and emotional support needed to start a new life. They also found an existing service delivery system which had experience in handling Indochinese refugees. Many earlier refugees now serve as educators, translators, social workers, or even sponsors of their own people. In some areas, more than 80 percent of the newly arrived refugees have been sponsored by former refugees. The number of Indochinese sponsors has reportedly increased quite rapidly in recent times, and these sponsors seem to be able to provide better services and help because they themselves were refugees not long ago. Not only can they better come to grips with the resettlement problems of the newly arrived refugees, but they can also understand and communicate more effectively with their own people than American sponsors can. Therefore, efforts should be made to encourage and boost this self-help trend.

The new refugees, therefore, seem to be better prepared psychologically to start a new life and enjoy some degree of psychological, social and economic security of which their predecessors were deprived.

The birth of some 500 so-called Indochinese mutual assistance associations throughout the U.S. is a clear indication of a need for a sense of belonging and for protection and social interactions. In terms of administration, resources, and objectives, most of these organizations are better described as social groups because their members and leadership are generally comprised of a few friends or acquaintances, and they are not very active due to lack of resources and/or regular staff. They usually meet once or twice a year on special occasions, providing some sort of social gatherings or cultural entertainments. However, there are a few associations set up and run by the Indochinese themselves which are active in meeting the needs of not only their own people but also of those non-Indochinese who have been or are working with Indochinese refugees. One of these viable organizations is the National Association for Vietnamese American Education, known as NAVAE. With a present membership of more than 500 professionals and paraprofessionals, this organization has been providing a variety of services at nominal or no cost to whomever needs them and has organized annual national conferences. In addition to a good number of non-Indochinese professionals and sponsors who work with Indochinese refugees, NAVAE has been able to rally the support of most, if not all, of the best known scholars and professionals from Vietnam. Due to the seemingly discriminatory funding practices and patterns by federal and state agencies in favor of non-Indochinese agencies and organizations, the vast resources and talents of Indochinese professionals and organizations have not been tapped and/or exploited yet. According to feedback from many Indochinese refugees, some of the resettlement agencies do not seem to be genuinely interested in helping refugees, but instead are only interested in receiving funding. As a result, there has been much resentment among Indochinese refugees against these agencies, and one has witnessed a number of poor quality programs which have been run by non-Indochinese whose services were ineffective in meeting the needs of the refugees.

Because of their cultural and socio-political backgrounds and experiences, the Indochinese are, by and large, not ones for organizing. Traditionally, they are not familiar with or active in organizations and pressure groups. At this point in time, they are still unable to have their voices heard on the national, regional, and local scene. They also seem unable to organize to defend their interests in this culturally diversified society. They should follow the examples set by their Asian predecessors, namely the Japanese Americans or other ethnic minority groups, such as American Jews and Italians, who have been able to influence federal, state, and local governments to serve their needs and to achieve political gains. With backgrounds and past experiences based upon the support of the family unit instead of political organizations or pressure groups, it will take much more time for the Indochinese to get organized. This process will certainly be shortened if something dramatic happens to them or their communities—if it is obvious to them that their interests and welfare are threatened or in jeopardy.

In summary, as one of the most adaptable and hard-working ethnic groups to have come to this country, and equipped with many advantages over earlier Asian immigrants, the majority of the Indochinese immigrants should be able to mainstream and become middle-class citizens within a comparatively shorter period of time than other Asian-American immigrant groups. The Indochinese Americans are law-abiding and contributing members of the American society. In addition to their talents and skills, their most important and valuable contribution of all is, perhaps, the 4,000 years of cultural and linguistic heritage that they have brought with them to add to this already culturally and linguistically rich country.

SELECTED LIST OF RESOURCE AND SERVICE CENTERS FOR INDOCHINESE POPULATION IN THE U.S.

Because they have Indochinese professionals on their staffs, the majority of the centers listed below can provide Indochinese materials and/or technical assistance, along with referral and training services to those who work with the Indochinese in the U.S. Since these centers are funded by public monies, their services and/or existence depend on the availability of public funds.

BABEL, Inc.
  (Bay Area Bilingual Education
  League, Inc.)
255 E. 14th St.
Oakland, CA 94606
(415) 451-0511

Bilingual Education Service
  Center
Georgetown University
35-20 Prospect St., N.W.
Washington, DC 20007
(202) 625-3540

Bilingual Education Service
  Center
Institute of Cultural Pluralism
San Diego State University
Sand Diego, CA 92182
(714) 265-5193

Bilingual Resource Center
7703 N. Lamar
Austin, TX 78752
(512) 458-9131

Center for Applied Linguistics
3520 Prospect St., N.W.
Washington, DC 20007
(202) 298-9292

Center for Southeast Asian
  Studies
Northern Illinois University
Dekalb, IL 60015
(815) 753-1771

Comprehensive Educational
  Assistance Center
California State University
800 N. State College Blvd.
Fullerton, CA 92634
(714) 773-3994

Cross-Cultural Resource Center
California State University
6000 J St.
Sacramento, CA 95819
(916) 454-6236

Indochinese Materials Center
324 E. 11th St.
Kansas City, MO 64106
(816) 374-3976

Intercultural Development
   Research Association
5835 Callaghan Rd.
San Antonio, TX 78231
(512) 684-8180

MERIT Bilingual Center
Temple University
Ritter Annex, Rm. 995
Philadelphia, PA 19122
(215) 787-6258

Mid-America Center for
   Bilingual Materials
   Development (MAC)
University of Iowa
N. 310 Oakdale Campus
Oakdale, IA 52319
(319) 353-5400

Midwest Resource Center for
   Bilingual Education
500 S. Dwyer Ave.
Arlington Heights, IL 60005
(312) 870-4100

National Association for
   Vietnamese American
   Education (NAVAE)
1123 Beverly Rd.
Jenkintown, PA 19046
(215) 572-5709

National Bilingual Resource
   Center
University of Southwestern
   Louisiana
P.O. Box 43410
Lafayette, LA 70504
(318) 264-6991

National Clearinghouse for
   Bilingual Education
1300 Wilson Blvd.
Suite B2-11
Rosslyn, VA 22209
(703) 522-0710 or
(800) 336-4560 (toll free)

REFERENCES

1. It should be noted that the principal sources of statistical data used in this paper are derived from the *Reports to the Congress* prepared by the U.S. Department of Health, Education and Welfare, between June 15, 1976 and December 31, 1979. 1980 census figures for specific ethnic groups are not yet available.

2. American Public Welfare Association, *Refugee Report* (March 26, 1982). Published under a grant from the U.S. Office of Refugee Resettlement, Department of Health and Human Services.

3. Post-1979 figures are not available.
4. The Source for Table 1 is the U.S. Department of Health and Human Services, U.S. Office of Refugee Resettlement.

BIBLIOGRAPHY

Allen, Virginia French. "Contributions of Indochinese-Speaking Teachers to ESL Programs." Paper presented in response to a request by Dr. Vuong G. Thuy, President of the National Association for Vietnamese American Education (NAVAE). This paper appeared in the *NAVAE Newsletter,* Vol. 1, No. 2, October 1980.

American Public Welfare Association, *Refugee Report,* 2 (19) (March 6, 1981).

Burmark, Lynell, and Hyung-Chan Kim. "The Challenge of Educating Vietnamese Children in American Schools," *Integrated Education* 16 (1) (January-February 1978): 2–8.

The Cambodian, Lao and Vietnamese Ways of Life." Anonymous and undated.

Carlin, Jean E. "Don't Expect Gratitude," unpublished, 1977.

"Indochinese Children and Families: An Overview." Research Capsule No. 4, Northwest Regional Child Welfare Training Center, School of Social Work, University of Washington, May 15, 1980.

Indochinese Refugees Adjustment Problems, Mental Health Projects for Indochinese Refugees, Oklahoma City, OK: Vietnamese American Association, 1979.

Khoa, Le Xuan. "Indochinese Mutual Assistance Organizations as Mechanisms in Community Mental Health." Paper presented at the National Conference on Social Welfare, 107th Annual Forum and Exhibits Program, May 18–21, 1980, Cleveland, OH.

———. "Vietnamese Immigrants and Their Adjustment to American Society." Paper presented at the Conference for IRAP Grantees and Contractors, D.H.E.W. Region II, April 1979, Brookdale Community College, Lincroft, NJ.

Montero, Darrell. "Vietnamese Refugees in America: Toward a Theory of Spontaneous International Migration," *International Migration Review* 13 (4) (Winter 1979): 624–48.

Starr, Paul D., et al. "Stressful Life Events and Mental Health Among Vietnamese Refugees: Inoculation and Synchronization." Paper presented at the Southern Sociological Society Annual Meetings, March 29, 1980, Knoxville, TN.

Thu, Nguyen Dinh. "Mutual Assistance Association's Role in Refugee Resettlement." Unpublished, 1980.

Thuy, Vuong G. "America: The Salad Bowl of the World." Keynote speech delivered at the 38th Annual Conference of the Oklahoma Health and Welfare Association, October 19-21, 1980, Tulsa, OK.

———. *Bilingual Education: A Necessity or a Luxury?* Palo Alto, CA: R. & E. Research Associates, Inc., 1979.

———. "Contrasts between Vietnamese and American Education: An Overview." Unpublished, December 1980.

———. *Getting to Know the Vietnamese and Their Culture.* New York: Frederick Ungar Publishing Co, 1976.

———. "The Needs and Expectations of the Indochinese in America." Keynote speech delivered at the First National Conference on Indochinese Education and Social

Services, organized by the National Association for Vietnamese American Education (NAVAE), March 28–29, 1980, Arlington, VA. ERIC document ED 191–966.

————. *Vietnamese in a Nutshell*, Montclair, NJ: Institute for Language Study, 1975.

Tri, Nguyen Quoc. "Culture and Technical Assistance in Public Administration. A Study of What Can Be Transferred from the United States to Vietnam." Unpublished Ph.D. diss., University of Southern California, 1970.

U.S. Department of Health, and Human Services. Report to Congress. The following issues were consulted: June 15, 1976; September 20, 1976; December 20, 1976; March 21, 1977; June 20, 1977; December 31, 1977; December 31, 1978; December 31, 1979; and March 26, 1982.

Wright, Jackie Bong. "Difficulties Encountered by Indochinese Refugees." Paper presented before the Mental Health Professionals, Mount Vernon Mental Health Center, November 6, 1979, Fairfax County, VA.

————. "Indochinese Refugee Children and Related Needs." Paper presented at the Fairfax County School Board Public Budget Hearing, January 28, 1980.

————. "Perspectives on American Blacklash against Indochinese Refugees." Paper presented at the Asian and Pacific Federal Employee Council, September 25, 1979, Washington, DC.

The Status of Native Hawaiian Education

by Bella Zi Bell

INTRODUCTION

There is no written history from ancient days to describe the migration of the Polynesian ancestors of the Hawaiians, but archeologists have determined by radiocarbon dating of ancient campsites that the earliest human habitation in the Hawaiian chain occurred from about 500 to 750 A.D. It is believed that the first settlers may have come from the Marquesas and that Tahitians may have arrived between 900 and 1300 A.D.

The early inhabitants of Hawaii developed a distinctive Stone Age culture over a period of about 1,000 years. Although they had neither written language nor metals, they established a subsistence economy with complex religious, cultural, and social practices. Theirs was a cooperative society in which natural resources were used with care and life was maintained in harmony with the environment.

Some 200 years ago, Captain James Cook and his crew encountered the hospitable Hawaiians and permanently altered the course of civilization on these islands. An estimate of the population in 1778, made by Captain Cook's officers, varied from 250,000–400,000 people.

The coming of Westerners had a fatal impact on the Hawaiians. Although foreigners made many contributions to the society, such as a written language, Western education, metal, and manufactured goods, they also introduced previously unknown diseases, firearms, and alcohol. The Western culture also produced complex changes in religion, land use, the economy, and health practices that permanently altered the Hawaiian culture. These and other factors led to the rapid depopulation of the Hawaiian race.[1]

In 1900, the first United States census taken in the Hawaiian Islands showed a count of 29,799 full Hawaiians and 7,857 part-Hawaiians.

Subsequent U.S. decennial censuses have shown the pure Hawaiians declining as a result of low fertility, high mortality, out-migration and intermarriage, while the number of part-Hawaiians has increased, as shown by the following percentages of Hawaiians and part-Hawaiians in the total population from 1900 to 1960:[2]

	1900	1910	1920	1930	1940	1950	1960
Hawaiians	19.3%	13.6%	9.3%	6.1%	3.4%	2.5%	1.8%
Part-Hawaiians	5.1	6.5	7.0	7.7	11.8	14.8	14.4

In the 1970 U.S. decennial census, the part-Hawaiian category was deleted, resulting in a count of 71,375 in the Hawaiian category, or 9.3 percent of Hawaii's total population. This change in categorization resulted in data that were lacking in comparability with both earlier U.S. census tabulations and the data series developed by the state of Hawaii. Therefore, it is difficult to determine ethnic population trends or to calculate valid rates for socioeconomic indicators by Hawaiian and part-Hawaiian ethnicity using 1970 census data. Subsequent U.S. Census Bureau surveys to update the 1970 data followed the 1970 census definition and procedures for ethnicity. And the 1980 U.S. Census has not reinstated the part-Hawaiian category. Thus, the inability to use census results in calculating various socioeconomic rates persists.

In view of the difficulties in using census data for Hawaiians and part-Hawaiians, this paper will use 2 State of Hawaii data sources: the Office of Economic Opportunity's *Census Update Survey of 1975* (which is the most recent comprehensive survey available on Hawaiians and part-Hawaiians) and the 1979 *State Health Surveillance Survey* data for update. Educational and socioeconomic data used are for the most recent year for which valid statistics are available.*

Demographic Characteristics

In 1979, there were 175,000 Hawaiians and part-Hawaiians (hereafter referred to as Native Hawaiians**) in the total resident population of

_____·

*Service agencies usually do not categorize their data by Hawaiians and part-Hawaiians. Where such data are available, the definitions used by various agencies may differ.

**Definition according to Public Law 93-644, Section 813: Native Hawaiian means any individual any of whose ancestors were natives of the area which consists of the Hawaiian islands prior to 1778.

880,000 in the state of Hawaii. The geographic distribution by island was as follows:

	Hawaii	Kauai	Maui	Molokai	Lanai	Oahu
Total population	9.4%	4.0%	6.3%	0.8%	0.3%	79.2%
Native Hawaiians	15.7	4.1	7.2	2.3	0.3	70.4

More than 52 percent of this Native Hawaiian population were 19 years of age or younger, whereas the state total population showed 35 percent aged 19 and under. Thus, the age structure for the Native Hawaiian population resembled that of developing countries where the percentage of children is larger than that of adults. On the other hand, the age structure for the total state population resembled that of developed countries, with a much smaller percentage of children. The socioeconomic characteristics of Native Hawaiians have also reflected those of developing countries where a larger proportion of children in the population are dependent on a smaller proportion of income-producing adults. For example, the following comparisons give an indication. of the socioeconomic status of Native Hawaiians in 1975:

	Native Hawaiian	State
Percent of population poor	23.9	11.3
Percent eligible for welfare	22.0	15.0
Percent in professional/technical managerial occupations	19.0	27.3
Unemployment rate (adults)	6.0	3.9

With a proportionately larger Native Hawaiian children and youth population, the proportion of Native Hawaiian students in the public school system has been similarly larger.

Characteristics of Native Hawaiian Students

Of the 162,000 public school students in the state in 1979, 34,000 (21 percent) were Native Hawaiian. Of 224 public schools in the State, 34 (15 percent) had enrollments of 40 percent or more Native Hawaiian. However, of the 8,000 public school teachers, only 6 percent were Native Hawaiian. Although about 22 percent of the youth in the state aged 18 to 21 were Native Hawaiian, of the community college students in the state, only 6 percent were Native Hawaiian. And only 4 percent of those studying at 4-year colleges statewide were Native Hawaiian.

It is true that the number of public school students in the state has declined in the past few years. But the number of Native Hawaiian students has remained about the same since 1977, due mainly to the fact that the total fertility rate for Native Hawaiians has been much higher than for the total state population (6122 versus 2729 per 1000 women in 1970).[3] In fact, proportionately, Native Hawaiian students have increased from 20 percent of the state student enrollment in 1977 to 21 percent in 1980. On the other hand, Native Hawaiian teachers have remained at about 6 percent of the total number of public school teachers. Since Native Hawaiian students make up more than one-fifth of the student enrollment, there should be an effort to increase the proportion of Native Hawaiian teachers or, at least, to train existing teachers in understanding how to teach Native Hawaiian children and how to teach in programs geared to bicultural/multicultural students who need special education.

EDUCATIONAL PROGRAMS TO MEET THE NEEDS OF NATIVE HAWAIIAN STUDENTS

In order to see which are the best special programs to meet the needs of Native Hawaiian students, their educational status should be presented. Available data indicate basic problems such as low achievement test scores, high absenteeism, high dropout rate, and general disciplinary problems.

Annually, the state Department of Education administers the Stanford Achievement Test (SAT) to fourth and eighth graders statewide. Recent results of the SAT for fourth graders showed that 34 percent of the Native Hawaiian students fell in stanines 1, 2, and 3 (below average) in reading, compared to 24 percent for all ethnic groups combined. For the eighth graders, the percentages were 44 percent versus 23 percent.[4]

Of the approximately 5,000 students in the 34 schools which had enrollments of 40 percent or more Native Hawaiian in 1979, 33 percent of these students were absent 20 or more days in the school year compared to 20 percent for all students. Some 25 percent of these students were absent 70 days or more out of a 173-day school year. These students can essentially be considered dropouts.[5] In 1979 also, of the 16,566 Native Hawaiian students enrolled in the State's intermediate and high schools, 8 percent (1,250) were suspended one or more times during the year, compared to half that percentage for all other ethnic groups combined.[6]

In view of these indicators, what is being offered in the way of alternative special education programs to meet the needs of these students?

Major State Compensatory Education Programs to Meet the Needs of the Educationally Disadvantaged

Title I Programs.[7] These are federally-funded programs under the provisions of the Elementary and Secondary Education Act of 1965 (ESEA). The goal is to assist disadvantaged students in overcoming their special educational, social, economic, and related difficulties which impede normal academic and personal progress in school. The objectives of Title I in the Hawaii public school system are to provide supplemental help in reading, mathematics, and, in some cases, preschool enrichment and readiness, and to place a strong emphasis on parental involvement.

Title I program results are measured in normal curve equivalents (NCE). A zero NCE means that the amount of learning was exactly what would have been expected had there been no Title I program. When an NCE gain is greater than zero, it means that the students profited from participating in the Title I program. In the period from 1977–80, the programs of the majority of the 50 schools which had 30 percent or more Hawaiians in their enrollment showed successful impact. Except for 7 schools, the schools showed NCE gains from 3.9 to 15.1. Thus, the Title I scores have indicated progress in the basic skills for students in these schools.

Comprehensive Mathematics Project.[8] (Complete name is The Improvement of School Programs in Mathematics through a Comprehensive Foundation Program Assessment and Improvement System [FPAIS] Approach Project.) The program's objective is the reduction of mathematics program deficiencies, as identified through state-level assessments, including problem-solving, applications in everyday situations, alertness to logical results, estimation and approximation, geometry, measurement, predictions, and interpreting and constructing tables, charts, and graphs. While the program is too new (it began in 1978) to fully evaluate its impact, the Stanford Achievement Test scores on math for 1979 and 1980 were the best ever for those grades which participated in the program.

Federal Right to Read Program.[9] Since 1975, the objective of this program has been to develop and utilize a statewide network of specially trained district teams to assist classroom teachers in reading improvement efforts. Emphasis is placed on overall reading comprehension skills rather than on reading mechanisms. The program has the Anne Adams Approach which teaches reading and writing skills by using materials that are available to students such as nonfiction books, newspapers, catalogs, and vocabulary from television shows. An integrated approach is emphasized, combining oral language, reading, and writing skills, and relying on group work and peer learning methods. Evaluations of this program at 35 schools have indicated that they have had a significant and educationally meaningful impact on the reading performance of the students. Most teachers and parents who have been involved in the program have been very pleased with the results.

Effect of State Compensatory Programs on Native Hawaiian Students

Despite the relatively positive evaluation of these programs, it is doubtful that they alone can resolve the special needs of Native Hawaiian students. One difficulty is that, under the criteria of these programs, many Native Hawaiian students who do not qualify as low-income, neglected, or handicapped and yet who do have major educational difficulties are not being serviced. Those students not enrolled in any type of compensatory education program and doing poorly in school are an unserviced gap group.[10] Another problem with these programs is that they reflect a high degree of remedial instruction using traditional teaching approaches. Cultural differences, attitudes, and expectations between the school's tradition and the Hawaiian culture are not addressed.[11] A less apparent difficulty is that some teachers may have low expectations of Native Hawaiian students and may not guide them sufficiently to remedy their academic weaknesses in order to pursue higher education and professions.

In view of these difficulties, private Hawaiian agencies and institutions have implemented innovative experimental programs which incorporate Hawaiian culture, values, and concepts and reconcile them with the educational process.

INNOVATIVE EDUCATION PROGRAMS TO MEET THE NEEDS OF NATIVE HAWAIIAN STUDENTS

Of the innovative experimental education programs for Native Hawaiians in the state, 2 have been evaluated as most successful. The first and most well-known is the Kamehameha Early Education Program (KEEP), a program of the Kamehameha Schools/Bishop Estates. The goal of KEEP is the development, demonstration, and dissemination of methods for improving the education of Native Hawaiian children. KEEP is the result of an interdisciplinary approach which combines contributions from anthropologists, linguistics, clinical and experimental psychologists, educators, and others. Its activities involve not only the traditional educational process but also bicultural teacher training, curriculum development, child motivation, language, and cognitive development. Its success has been demonstrated through cohort analysis by a time experiment comparing KEEP students with similar control groups. For each grade level, the experimental group exceeded its controls in all basic skills with statistically significant difference.

The Pahoa School Program of the Queen Liliuokalani Children's Center includes various educational and cultural components to help Native Hawaiian children. The objective is to involve the parents and the community in modifying traditional education methods with Hawaiian history, culture, and recreation. Evaluation of this program, through the Stanford Achievement Test, has shown that students in the program score higher than both the state and the national averages.

Other small, short-term demonstration programs to enrich the education of Native Hawaiian students have proven successful, according to test results. One has been Program Ho'aloha; its objective was to have students become aware, and be proud, of their Hawaiian cultural heritage, to appreciate other ethnic groups and their contributions to Hawaii, and to receive remedial instruction in the basic skills. Other successful programs have included the ALU LIKE Halau O Haleiwa program, the Early Prevention of School Failure Program, and the Hui Laulima Program.

It seems that those programs that have been most successful are programs for preschool and elementary school age children. Researchers believe that young children who are turned off early in elementary school and are chronically absent are likely to develop antisocial behavior as adolescents. In summary, evaluation studies indicate that, to raise the skill levels of Native Hawaiian students, the following provisions must be made in order for special programs to be successfully implemented:

1. Reaching out to students early to instill in them an appreciation of their bi/multiculturalism.
2. Making students feel comfortable about themselves; raising their self-esteem as well as their cognitive skills.
3. Making any task practical, i.e., learning by doing, while tying in basic skills.
4. Involving parents or other support systems that will provide reinforcement and encouragement in the home environment—especially important for Native Hawaiian children who appear to need more continued motivation.[12]
5. Involving Native Hawaiian professionals and leaders in the community who can become role models for Native Hawaiian children and encouraging them to pursue higher education and professions.

In view of the favorable outcome of these present and past special demonstration programs for Native Hawaiian children, it seems such programs should be implemented in the state public school system. Unfortunately, there is the problem of funding. Demonstration programs operating on special funds often are not picked up by the public school system as part of its regular program because to do so would require replication of the programs throughout the state to ensure equal opportunity for all students. Because this would be much more expensive than the present education system can absorb, alternative means need to be sought, which will ensure that special programs focusing on Native Hawaiian student needs will continue.

FINANCIAL ASSISTANCE FOR THE EDUCATION OF NATIVE HAWAIIANS

A major alternative means for funding Native Hawaiian education programs is the proposed Native Hawaiian Education Act, which would seek federal funds for special programs for Native Hawaiians, commensurate with their status as Native Americans. The federal government has traditionally maintained a special relationship with Native Hawaiians and has dealt with them in a manner similar to that of other Native Americans.[13] In 1920, the Solicitor of the U.S. Department of the Interior and the Attorney General for the Territory of Hawaii rendered similar opinions that Congress had the same power to enact legislation for Native Hawaiians as it had for the benefit of American Indians and Alaskans. In the Admissions Act of 1959, Congress reaffirmed its trust responsibility to Native Hawaiians by mandating the State of Hawaii to recognize the Hawaiian Homes Commission Act. In 1974, Congress reiterated its special relationship with Native Hawaiians through amended legislation which included them as eligible for national programs administered by the Administration for Native Americans, Office of Human Development Services, U.S. Department of Health, Education, and Welfare (now the Department of Health and Human Services). The process was repeated in 1977 when Congress amended the Employment and Training Act to include Native Hawaiians in the Native American Manpower Program which was administered by the U.S. Department of Labor through the Division of Indian and Native American Programs.

In view of the precedents established by these congressional actions and the availability of comparable services to other indigenous Native Americans, the enactment of educational programs designed to meet the unique needs of Native Hawaiians is justified.

In 1979, the Native Hawaiian Education Bill (S. 916) was introduced by Senators Daniel K. Inouye and Spark M. Matsunaga of Hawaii to the First Session of the 96th Congress. In brief, the bill summarized the educational needs of Native Hawaiians and proposed the following.[14]

Improvement of Educational Opportunities for Native Hawaiian Children

1. To plan for and take steps leading to the development of programs specifically designed to meet the special educational, or culturally related academic needs, or both, of Native Hawaiian children, including pilot projects designed to test the effectiveness of plans so developed.
2. To establish, maintain, and operate programs—including remodeling of classrooms or other space used for the programs and acquisitions of necessary equipment—specially designed to meet the special education and culturally related academic needs, or both, of Native Hawaiian children.
3. To possibly include the participation of non-Native Hawaiian children in a program or project where that participation does not frustrate or inhibit the achievement of the purpose of the program.
4. To plan a program in open consultation with parents of Native Hawaiian children enrolled in the affected schools, with teachers of those children, and, where applicable, with Native Hawaiian secondary school students, including public hearings at which time such persons have a full opportunity to understand the program and to offer recommendations thereon; a program should also have the participation and approval of a committee composed of, and selected by, the above groups.
5. To support demonstration projects which are designed to test and demonstrate the effectiveness of programs for improving educational opportunities for Native Hawaiian children.
6. To assist in the establishment and operation of programs which are designed to stimulate the provision of educational services not available to Native Hawaiian children in sufficient quantity or quality; to develop and establish exemplary educational programs to serve as models for regular school programs in which Native Hawaiian children are educated.
7. To encourage the dissemination of information and materials relating to, and to evaluate the effectiveness of, education programs which may offer educational opportunities to Native Hawaiian children, including:
   a. innovative programs related to the education needs of educationally deprived children;
   b. bilingual and bicultural education programs and projects;

c. special health and nutrition services and other related activities which meet the special health, social and psychological problems of Native Hawaiian children;
d. coordination of the operation of other federally assisted programs which may be used to assist in meeting the needs of such children;
e. remedial and compensatory instruction, school health, physical education, psychological and other services designed to assist and encourage Native Hawaiian children to enter, remain in, or reenter elementary or secondary school;
f. comprehensive academic and vocational instruction;
g. comprehensive guidance, counseling, and testing services;
h. special education programs for handicapped and gifted and talented Native Hawaiian children;
i. early childhood programs; and
j. exemplary and innovative educational programs and centers which involve new educational approaches, methods, and techniques designed to enrich programs of elementary and secondary education.

Special Education Training Programs for Teachers of Native Hawaiian Children

1. To fund training for the purpose of preparing individuals for teaching or administering special programs and projects designed to meet the special educational needs of Native Hawaiian children and to provide in-service training for persons teaching in such programs, including fellowships and traineeships.
2. To award fellowships to Native Hawaiian students to enable them to pursue a course of study for 4 academic years which lead toward a professional or graduate degree in medicine, law, education, and related fields or which lead to an undergraduate or graduate degree in engineering, business administration, natural resources, and related fields.

Improvement of Education Opportunities for Adult Native Hawaiians

1. To support demonstration projects which are designed to test and demonstrate the effectiveness of programs for improving employment and educational opportunities for adult Native Hawaiians.
2. To assist in the establishment and operation of programs which are designed to stimulate the provision of basic literacy opportunities to all nonliterate Native Hawaiian adults and the provision of opportunities to all Native Hawaiian adults so they may qualify for high school equivalency certificates in the shortest period of time feasible.

3. To support a major research and development program to develop more innovative and effective techniques for achieving literacy and high school equivalency goals.
4. To provide for basic surveys and evaluations thereof to define accurately the extent of the problems of illiteracy and of high school completion among Native Hawaiians.
5. To encourage the dissemination of information and materials relating to, and the evaluation of, the effectiveness of educational programs which may offer opportunities to Native Hawaiian adults.
6. To establish an advisory council on Native Hawaiian Education to oversee the administration of the provisions in this Bill.

Unfortunately, there has been inadequate positive response to this proposed bill. There is indifference due to the lack of understanding of the Native Hawaiian people, lack of knowledge of the socioeconomic and educational status of the Native Hawaiians, and lack of data explaining why existing federal special education programs are not meeting the needs of Native Hawaiians.

Fortunately, the 1980 Congress did pass legislation in September 1980 to set up an advisory council on Native Hawaiian education. The council was authorized by Section 1331 of the Education Amendments of 1980 (P.L. 96-374, 10 U.S.C. 1221-1), which states that (1) like other Native Americans, Native Hawaiians rank among the lowest in level of educational attainment and per capita income, and (2) existing federal, state, and local assistance in the field of education fails to address the basic and special needs of Native Hawaiians. Thus Congress declares its commitment to assist in providing the educational services and opportunities that Native Hawaiians need.

The council shall advise the U.S. secretary of education, the assistant secretary for elementary and secondary education, and other appropriate officials regarding the operation of programs administered by the department and other programs making educational assistance available to Native Hawaiians. It will submit a report to the secretary and to the Congress no later than January 31, 1983, containing its findings and recommendations.

ADVISORY COUNCIL ON NATIVE HAWAIIAN EDUCATION

The 7 members of this council have been appointed by the U.S. secretary of education after consultation with the governor of Hawaii. Its mission and goals follow below.[15]

Mission

" . . . Existing federal, state, and local assistance fails to address satisfactorily the educational needs of Native Hawaiians. . . . The task of this Advisory Council is to consider reasons why this condition exists and to recommend to the Secretary of Education, and the Congress, legislative and administrative remedies. Said remedies could have expanded benefits as they may prove to be applicable to other Native Americans and other Polynesians in assisting them to attain educational parity with groups represented in the social mainstream."

Goals

1. Validate that Native Hawaiians do not achieve at parity in education.
    a. Present achievement test score data.
    b. Present socioeconomic indicator data.
    c. Identify the number of at-risk individuals along the age continuum.
    d. Describe the residual effects of the problem and the relationship to future generations of Native Hawaiians.
    e. Locate the at-risk population and identify impacted communities.
2. Delineate the special health, social and psychological needs of Native Hawaiian children that appear to underlie this condition.
    a. Present evidence that Native Hawaiians experienced bodily and psychological trauma that undermined their physical and emotional health.
    b. Present evidence that there is a causal relationship between physical and emotional health and low educational achievement.
3. Inventory and evaluate existing federal, state and local assistance that intends to remedy the condition.
    a. Identify federal, state and local programs that are designed to remedy the problem.
    b. Define criteria for measuring cost-effective, successful program.
    c. Evaluate federal, state and local programs that are designed to remedy the problem.
    d. List areas of educational need that are not being met by existing programs.
4. Highlight educational approaches that seem to be most effective in remedying the conditions.
    a. Identify existing programs that are successful remedies.
    b. Identify existing remedies with potential for replication or expansion.
    c. Identify areas of continuing need for program development.

5. Recommend to the Secretary of Education and the Congress appropriate legislative and administrative remedies.
   a. Submit recommendations to the Congress.
   b. Submit recommendations to the Secretary of Education.
   c. Submit recommendations to interested Native American and Polynesian groups.

BENEFITS TO SOCIETY FROM EDUCATIONAL INVESTMENT

As has been shown, compared to the total population of Hawaii, Native Hawaiians are a disadvantaged people who need special educational assistance. Even if lawmakers might be convinced of this fact, however, they would probably pose the question: "Will there be a sufficient return on the dollar investment that may produce benefits to society beyond those immediately apparent to the recipients of funds, thereby making this appropriation a particularly good use of public funds?" A study analyzing the costs and benefits of educational achievement as it relates to employment income presents the following.[16]

For each additional year of schooling completed, an individual Native Hawaiian's average income rose by over $700 per year in 1975. Does this gain in income represent an adequate rate of return to society to justify the expenditures to provide that education? By inducing a potential high school dropout to finish high school, society reaps dividends (over additional educational costs) in the amount of 16 percent for part-Hawaiians and 30 percent for Hawaiians after accounting for inflation. These returns more than meet the market test of adequate returns which are in the range of 5 to 10 percent. Furthermore, in computing this rate of return to society, not included in the calculations are the cost savings due to lower welfare dependency rates and lower criminal offender rates associated with higher educational achievement. Calculated returns compare only the additional incomes gained by more education against the additional costs incurred by society to provide that education to Native Hawaiians. Thus, compared to alternative uses of society's capital, the returns to society from educational investment for Native Hawaiians are more than sufficient.

The case for the needs of the Native Hawaiians for special education has been documented. Fortunately, the 6 Hawaiian agencies and institutions entrusted to serve Native Hawaiians have joined together to voice their concerns to local, state, and national officials and to share ideas on how best to narrow this disparity in educational achievement and socioeconomic status. With continued joint effort, the realization of this goal will surely come to pass.

REFERENCES

1. Eleanor C. Nordyke, *The Peopling of Hawaii* (Honolulu, HI: The University Press of Hawaii, 1977), pp. 5–14.

2. Robert C. Schmitt, *Demographic Statistics of Hawaii, 1778–1965* (Honolulu, HI: University of Hawaii Press, 1968), p. 120.

3. Nordyke, Table 7.

4. Office of Program Evaluation and Planning, *Needs Assessment Update* (Honolulu, HI: The Kamehameha Schools, May 1981), p. 3.

5. Research and Statistics Unit, ALU LIKE, Inc., *A Report on Absenteeism in Public Schools Which Have 40% or More Native Hawaiian Students* (Honolulu, HI: ALU LIKE, Inc., July 1979), p. 12.

6. George K. Ikeda and James H. Jackson, *A Report on Educational, Employment and Training Needs of Native Hawaiian Youth* (Honolulu, HI: Research and Statistics Unit, ALU LIKE, Inc., April 1980), p. 61.

7. James H. Jackson, *A Report on Federal and State Supplemental Programs for Elementary Schools with High Concentrations of Hawaiian/ Part-Hawaiian Students* (Honolulu, HI: Research and Statistics Unit, ALU LIKE, Inc., December, 1980), pp. 101–22.

8. Jackson, pp. 101–22.

9. Jackson, pp. 101–22.

10. Myron B. Thompson, Neil J. Hannahs, and Hardy Spoehr, *Briefing Paper on the Native Hawaiian Education Act* (Honolulu, HI: Research and Statistics Unit, ALU LIKE, Inc., August 1979), p. 8.

11. George K. Ikeda, *A Report on Native Hawaiian Youth Employment and Training Needs* (Honolulu, HI: Research and Statistics Unit, ALU LIKE, Inc., March 1980), p. 39.

12. Ikeda and Jackson, pp. 14–19.

13. Thompson, Hannahs, and Spoehr, pp. 1–3.

14. *The Native Hawaiian Education Act,* Bill S.916, 96th Congress, 1st Session, Washington, DC, August 27, 1979, pp. 13–24.

15. *Planning Brief for the Advisory Council on Native Hawaiian Education* (Honolulu, HI: Advisory Council on Native Hawaiian Education, February, 1981), pp. 1–3.

16. James Mak and Edwin T. Fujii, *A Cost-Benefit Study Relating to the Native Hawaiian Education Act* (Honolulu, HI: Research and Statistics Unit, ALU LIKE, Inc., November 1979), pp. 6–8.

Index

Compiled by Linda Schexnaydre

$83028 1952